A Treasury of Civil War Humor

A Treasury of Civil War Humor

By

Sylvia G. L. Dannett

New York • THOMAS YOSELOFF • London

©1963 by A. S. Barnes and Company, Inc.
Library of Congress Catalog Card Number: 63-9378

Thomas Yoseloff, Publisher
8 East 36th Street
New York 16, N. Y.

Thomas Yoseloff Ltd.
18 Charing Cross Road
London W. C. 2, England

6035

Printed in the United States of America

For my son Kennie and my daughter Wendy
May Their Lives Be Filled with the Sound of Laughter
and
Not the Drumbeat of War

Foreword

During America's Civil War, as in times of stress during our more recent past, people sought release from their day-to-day tensions through laughter. Abraham Lincoln felt that he "should die" if he could not laugh, and was an enthusiast of both literary and graphic humor. On the day he was to present his Preliminary Emancipation Proclamation to his cabinet, he first read aloud to the members selections from the humorous writings of Artemus Ward.

As a result of the public's great need for laughter the early sixties witnessed an unprecedented outpouring of comic drawings and writings. These have been for the most part ignored by historians. Aside from an occasional nod to a Civil War cartoon no adequate recognition has been given to the humorists of a century ago despite the fact that their works present an important picture of the times. Contemporary comic valentines, cartoons, envelope illustrations, funny poems, and humorous literature tell their own story of the war and give us greater insight into the spirit of the people as well as the principles and ideals of the opposing sides.

The humor of the Civil War was distinctly native and indigenous. In the very early stages of the conflict it appeared on the surface to be almost folksy; at other times it had a homely unpretentious quality as if one member of a family were indulgently poking fun at a recalcitrant relative.

But before long the folksiness became a mere screen for verbal barbs, and the attitude of brother toward brother grew increasingly derisive and bitter.

In those days as in our time, Americans loved to laugh at themselves. Again and again cartoons depict a reluctance to be drafted and the difficulties of recruitment. Southern Limericks lampoon Southern generals for their failure to win a battle, and Northern lyrics satirize the weaknesses of leaders in their own ranks. This self-laughter and self-ridicule oftentimes misled foreign humorists, particularly French cartoonists, into believing that there was no difference in the motives and goals for which each side was fighting.

American humorists, however, were perhaps more realistic. Their humor did not serve simply to amuse the public, but was frequently a means of stirring up patriotism, sending out danger signals, or inspiring more active participation in the war effort. Lincoln considered the Nast cartoons in *Harper's Weekly* his best recruiting agent.

The amount of Civil War humor that has been bequeathed to us is so vast as to overwhelm the hardiest editor. Much of the wit is outmoded and dated and the references and allusions obscure. But a great deal of it is as alive and vital now as it was a hundred years ago. From this latter group I have chosen for this book such graphic and literary humor as appears the most truly representative and the funniest.

SYLVIA G. L. DANNETT

Scarsdale, New York
September 1, 1962

Acknowledgments

There are always a number of people who contribute toward the success of a book. I am particularly indebted to Miss Rachel Minick, Librarian of the New-York Historical Society, for her helpfulness in locating material for this book and for her editorial criticism; and to Mrs. Ernestine Arms who so faithfully typed and retyped this manuscript which, because of its format, required a great deal of detailed work.

To these others, also, I am very grateful for their assistance and interest: Dr. Julian Fahy, Washington, D.C., for his excellent researching of important materials; Sylvester Vigilante, Ossining, N.Y., for recommending and locating some of the reference books; Arnold Gates, Civil War Round Table of New York, for supplying necessary information; Preston Ewing, New York, advertising, for his advice and assistance on planning the format of the book; Dr. James Heslin, Director, New-York Historical Society, for his editorial criticism; Dr. John Cone, English Instructor, Scarsdale High School, for contributing a number of selections for the section on Lyrical Laughs; Mrs. Desi Kriete for her assistance in the typing of the book; Miss India Thomas, Regent, the Confederate Museum, Richmond; and the librarians of the Confederate Museum, the New-York Historical Society, the New York Public Library American History Room, and the Scarsdale Public Library, Scarsdale, N.Y.

Contents

A Treasury of Civil War Humor

I

Early Cartoons

A century ago a group of graphic humorists, armed with sketch pad and pencil, traced the entire course of the American Civil War on home and battlefront. They left us a heritage of cartoons which provides an excellent source for learning the social and political history of the period.

Pictorial histories have become increasingly popular as a means of viewing and studying the past, but it is the cartoon which truly conveys the essence, the bittersweet mood of the times. By its very tendency to deride, the political cartoon in particular points up —often ruthlessly—the fallacies, evils, and weaknesses of issues and people.

Originally all political cartoons, as well as satirical, grotesque, and humorous drawings, were called caricatures. The term caricature is said to be derived from the Italian *caricare*, meaning "to load." The art, therefore, according to Carl W. Drepperd, "has often been defined as 'overloaded representation' or laying it on too thick." Certainly this last may be applied to much of the nineteenth century graphic humor in the United States.

The term "cartoon" was first popularized in 1843 when, according to William Murrell, "*Mr. Punch,* taking a dig at the exhibition of artists' designs and studies for the decoration of the new houses of parliament, 'facetiously' called his principal political caricature a 'cartoon.'" After that, a distinction was made between the two types of humorous drawings. Murrell goes on further to define cartoons as a "forceful presentation by means of exaggeration of a topical, political, or moral issue, intended for a wide audience and making use of popular symbols and slogans." The caricature, on the other hand, by definition is a more subtle form of graphic art, a "satiric exposing of individual physical peculiarities and idiosyncrasies of manner, and its success depends wholly upon the psychological penetration of the artist."

15

As one of the oldest of the graphic arts, caricature can trace its humorous history back to the ancient Egyptian hieroglyphics and drawings on papyrus or frescoes.

As early as the thirteenth century, Jews were caricatured in England; many caricaturists attempted to ridicule Martin Luther. A caricature of Pope Julius II is attributed to Rabelais, and Leonardo da Vinci executed grotesques and caricatures.

In succeeding centuries, men continued to make their reputations in the field of satirical art by deriding public events, persons, or conditions of life which appealed to man's sense of humor, honor, justice or mercy. Hogarth, Cruikshank, Daumier, and other early draftsmen are still appreciated for their work in this field.

The first known caricature to appear in America was published by Benjamin Franklin in his *Pennsylvania Gazette* May 9, 1754, and roused the colonists to unite against their then common foe, the French and Indians. The Stamp Act and the Boston Tea Party inspired early caricaturists to play up anti-British feeling.

Paul Revere was one of the few caricaturists of the Revolutionary War period, and samples of his work are very rare. One of the best known is also on the subject of tea: "The Able Doctor; or America Swallowing the Bitter Draught."

Cartoons shed light on American folklore through the graphic development of our symbolic figures, Brother Jonathan, Major Jack Downing, and Uncle Sam. Early cartoonists symbolized America by a figure of a wild red Indian, a bucking horse, or an eagle. Then, sometime during the seventeen seventies, Brother Jonathan, the lank, shrewd, sharp, clever Yankee, first of America's symbolic figures, made his graphic appearance. Some consider Jonathan Trumbull, who died in 1783, the original of Brother Jonathan. Others trace the loutish Yankee hero's origin to the British-inspired "Yankee Doodle." The folk character next appeared in Royall Tyler's play *The Contrast* with such success that numerous plays followed which featured the stage Yankee. Constance Rourke finds the philosophy of nature "somehow flung around the spare figure of Yankee Jonathan" in the opera *The Forest Rose,* produced in 1825.

Uncle Sam is first mentioned during the War of 1812. Army supplies were packed and shipped by a man named Samuel Wilson, more familiarly known as "Uncle" Sam Wilson. Because the supplies were labeled "U.S.," word spread that "Uncle Sam" was feeding and taking care of the army. An interesting reference to this story appears in the *New York Gazette and General Advertiser,* May 12, 1830:

Immediately after the declaration of the last war with England, Elbert Anderson, Esq., of this city, then a Contractor, visited Troy, on the Hudson, where was concentrated, and where he purchased, a large quantity of provisions—beef, pork, etc. The inspectors of these articles at that place were Messrs. Ebenezer and Samuel Wilson. The latter gentleman (invariably known as "Uncle Sam") generally superintended in person a large number of workmen, who, on this occasion, were employed in overhauling the provisions purchased by the Contractor for the army. The casks were marked E.A.—U.S. The work fell to the lot of a facetious fellow in the employ of the Messrs. Wilsons [sic], who on being asked by some of his fellow workmen the meaning of the mark (for the letters U.S. for United States, was then almost entirely new to them) said, "he did not know, unless it meant Elbert Anderson and Uncle Sam"—alluding exclusively, then, to the said "Uncle Sam" Wilson. The joke took among the workmen, and passed currently; and "Uncle Sam" himself being present, was occasionally rallied by them on the increasing extent of his possessions.

Many of these workmen . . . were found shortly after following the recruiting drum, and pushing toward the frontier lines, for the double purpose of meeting the enemy, and of eating the provisions they had lately labored to put in good order. Their old jokes of course accompanied them, and before the first campaign ended, this identical one first appeared in print—it gained favor rapidly, till it penetrated and was recognized in every part of the country, and will no doubt continue so as long as U.S. remains a nation. . . .

From that time on, it was more or less understood that the symbolic figure, Uncle Sam, represented the collective head of the American household. His nephew, Jonathan, was more frequently seen before the fifties due to the influence of European cartoonists, particularly the British, who seemed to be partial to Yankee Jonathan.

In 1834 a cartoon, "Uncle Sam Sick with La Grippe," presented the symbolic figure in the form he was definitely to assume. This is said to be the only known cartoon in which Uncle Sam and Brother Jonathan are both depicted. Murrell believes that Brother Jonathan typified the people and Uncle Sam the nation.

In 1843 Edward W. Clay drew an Uncle Sam in eighteenth century costume, and thus he appeared later in two prints issued by Currier and Ives during the Presidential campaign of 1860: "Stephen Finds his Mother" and "Uncle Sam Making New Arrangements."

In the 1830's the third symbolic American character turned up in the cartoon world, Major Jack Downing. The Major first appeared in the *Letters of Major Jack Downing*, by Seba Smith, published in the early thirties. He then was presented in a series of cartoons by a draftsman or, it is believed, draftsmen, who signed themselves "Zek Downing, Neffu to Major Jack Downing." For many years Downing commented amusingly on the political affairs of the nation.

Over the years the figure of Brother Jonathan developed more and more into the familiar figure of Uncle Sam as we know him. Although both national symbols continued to appear in greater numbers through the Civil War period, by the early 1860's the name Uncle Sam was more popularly used. In *Vanity Fair* for April 20, 1861, the broad flat hat usually worn by Jonathan appeared on a rather youthful-looking Uncle Sam. However, Uncle Sam wore the striped trousers and starry vest associated with him. In 1861, in the cartoon "What on Earth Are You Doing to That Bird of Mine?," the symbolic figure came the closest to Uncle Sam as we know him of any cartoon published to that date. Finally, the two symbolic figures were merged and America's Uncle was represented as the stern, elderly gentleman with a tall stovepipe hat and the world-famous whiskers.

The nineteenth century became the great Cartoon Era in the United States, chiefly because of the establishment of commercial lithography in the eighteen twenties.

Early cartoons were pen or pencil drawings which were reproduced from wood, steel, or copper engravings. Where wood was used, the cartoons were either drawn directly on, or transferred to, blocks of boxwood. Skilled engravers then cut away all the wooden surface not covered by the lines of the drawing and the printing was done from the remaining design. This was such a lengthy process that many publishers employed a large staff of engravers. Full-page or double-page illustrations were divided into sections, each of which could be engraved by a different man. After the small blocks were engraved, they were locked together in a form from which the entire picture was printed as a unit.

Lithography involved neither cutting nor incising. The drawing was made directly on a properly prepared stone "of somewhat porous quality," with a greasy or oily substance.

After being treated by an acid to set the drawing on its surface, the stone was washed with water. Ink impressions were then taken from the stone as in ordinary printing.

As a result of this simplified method of reproduction, lithographed cartoons flooded the market. The razor-edged pencil of the graphic humorist commented sharply on the political scene during the Jacksonian era, the Mexican War, the acquisition of Texas, and the California gold rush. Graphic humorists can step in where writers might fear to tread since there is always a question as to whether a cartoon is to be taken seriously or laughed off as pure satire. Few articles could have pointed up so clearly and succinctly Andrew Jackson's predicament during the Peggy Eaton scandal as the cartoon "The Rats Leaving a Falling House," or the contempt the majority of Northerners felt toward the pro-Southern Copperheads during the Civil War as expressed in the Leland picture of a large reptile with the face of Clement Vallandigham, demigod of the movement.

As the mid-century approached, cartoonists found greater opportunities for marketing their pictures. First, there were comic almanacs patterned after Cruikshank's Almanac containing strictly Americana humor, which were well received by the public. Then a series of new newspapers appeared which featured pictures by some of the best known artists in the field. *Yankee Doodle* came off the press in 1846 with Charles Martin as its principal artist; Philadelphia's *John Donkey* in 1848 contained the work of Felix Octavius Carr Darley, and the short-lived *Lantern* made its debut in 1851 with drawings and cartoons by men like Bellew, Gunn, and Stephenson. England, of course, had *Punch, or the London Charivari,* founded in 1841, noted for its biting political cartoons by John Leech and John Tenniel. During the Mason and Slidell affair Tenniel's work was anything but pleasing to the North. "Do what's right, my son," the burly sailor John Bull admonished little Admiral Jonathan, in one cartoon, "or I'll blow you out of the water." Cham, the French cartoonist for *L'Illustration, Journal Universel,* emphasized consistently in his cartoons that he saw no difference between the Blues and Grays. His humor is more subtle than that found in the majority of American illustrated magazines.

The late fifties saw the birth of the future giants of the illustrated weekly field: *Harper's Weekly* in 1857, *Frank Leslie's* in 1858, and *Vanity Fair* in December, 1859. Frank Beard wielded a vigorous pen in his *Harper* drawings but it is Thomas Nast who is said to have made that weekly a political power before the close of the Civil War.

When war broke out, eighteen-year-old Nast was filled with a burning patriotism which found expression in powerful "emblematic pictures" that stirred the people and cheered the soldier. The power of his cartoons is attributed in large measure to a note of seriousness that dominated them.

Vanity Fair's artist Louis H. Stephens produced a number of devastating cartoons on Buchanan's do-nothing policy during the latter part of his administration, but Stephens really made his reputation as a graphic humorist in his cartoons of Lincoln.

Still another magazine came on the market during the war, very pointedly called *The Phunny Phellow,* which featured political comic strips as well as single cartoons, many by J. A. Read, who also did humorous cartoons for *Vanity Fair.*

The slavery issue, the Kansas Question, Harriet Beecher Stowe, and the Presidential campaign of 1856 were popular subjects for satirical art in the early fifties. Currier and Ives established their famous partnership in 1856 in time to produce some excellent cartoons satirizing Fremont in the Presidential campaign of that year. Cartoonists were stimulated to even greater productivity up and through the campaign of 1860, the election of Abraham Lincoln, secession, and finally the outbreak of the Civil War.

The past rises before us as we view the bloody struggle between Free Soil and pro-slavery advocates in Kansas with Pierce, Buchanan, Cass, Marcy, and Douglass depicted by the cartoonists as the true outlaws; rats with labels of Southern states fleeing from black cat "Uncle Abe" as secession gained in momentum; men being recruited for the armed forces; fair maidens wooing their beaux to war; soldiers marching gaily off to battle under waving banners.

Because there were greater opportunities for the graphic humorist in the North and along the eastern seaboard, the South produced few cartoonists in the ante-bellum days. "Porte Crayon," David Hunter Strother of Virginia, was a caricaturist of note, but he was primarily an illustrator.

It is unlikely that Southern historians would take pride in Strother's achievements since he fought on the Union side in the war. He first offered his services to the Governor of Virginia, but then is said to have become alarmed over the prospect of losing his gains as a writer and caricaturist in Northern journals. One female Southern diarist who considered Strother a "cowardly renegade" claims that the artist "went to the enemy because they offered him better pay and higher rank."

Manassas and other Southern victories did inspire Confederate cartoonists, but very little of their work has been preserved. The man considered the outstanding Southern cartoonist during the holocaust is Dr. Adalbert Johann Volck, a German-born Baltimore dentist and rabid Southern sympathizer. His *Confederate Etchings* faithfully express the spirit and convictions of the Southern people during the war years. To get ideas for these etchings, Volck repeatedly ran the blockade and is said to have acted as an agent of the Confederacy. Three of his drawings are especially directed at Lincoln, a popular target for Southern sympathizers. As a matter of precaution, Volck used the pseudonym V. Blada, the letters of his name in reverse, and the original etchings, thirty in number, were secretly made for private distribution during the war. Despite such secrecy, the United States government finally caught up with the dentist. His identity was established and he was arrested and imprisoned.

In 1863 the South produced its first magazine of humor, *Southern Punch*, but it did not have the lasting quality of its English parent, for after one year it closed shop.

As the war continued, the cartoons reflected the growing resentments, fierce animosities, and prejudices on both sides. The South, among other things, condemned the Northern civilization as materialistic, productive of hypocrisy, and full of "isms." The North generally had little to offer about the South except sensational and often unsubstantiated propaganda.

Behind the lines, people North and South were eager for news, whether it was brought to them in text or pictures. In the following pages the reader will follow the course of the war as it was seen through the eyes of the graphic humorists a century ago.

"THREE TO ONE YOU DON'T GET IT."

[VARIATION ON THE POPULAR INTERPRETATION OF THE MEANING OF THE PAWNBROKER'S SIGN.]

On September 1, 1860, Stephens pictures Lincoln carrying a load of rails labeled "Tribune Chicago Platform" and "Sambo the Slave Boy" into a pawnshop; the three balls of the shop are labeled "Douglas", "Breckenridge" and "Bell."

As the country took the road to war, graphic humorists caricatured the grim face of disaster. . . . Derisive scenes portrayed Republican determination not to compromise . . . While conditions worsened in Charleston harbor.

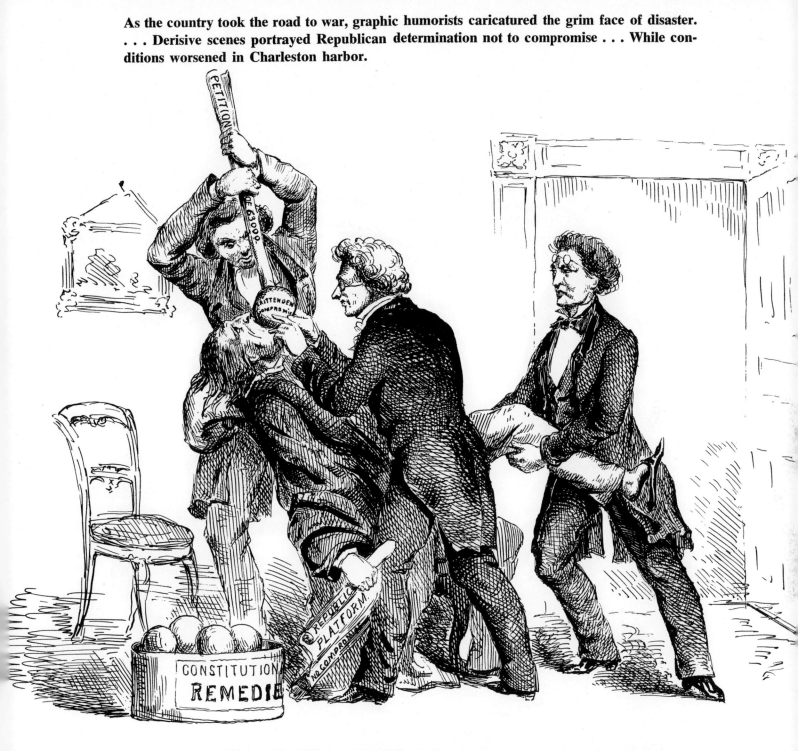

A CURE FOR REPUBLICAN LOCK-JAW

In this cartoon, the uncompromising attitude of the Republicans is emphasized. At the left a man, holding a paper, "Republican Platform, No Compromise," is having a huge pill labeled "Crittenden Compromise" forced down his throat by two men, one prodding with "Petition of 63000". A third man holds his leg. Behind the victim is a large box of pills labeled "Constitutional Remedies."

Senator John Crittenden of Kentucky recommended that all territory north of the southern boundary line of Missouri, running to the Pacific Ocean would be free soil forever, and all territory south of that line would be slave soil forever by Constitutional Amendment. The Constitution would declare that Congress was forbidden ever to abolish slavery or interfere with it in the slave states or in the District of Columbia. Slave owners would be paid by the Federal government for slave property lost through action of law courts in the North.

STEPHEN FINDING "HIS MOTHER."

This lithograph by Currier and Ives was drawn in 1860 by Louis Maurer. Columbia with Phrygian cap chastizes Douglas with cat, "Maine Law." Uncle Sam in eighteenth century costume says, "That's right! . . . give him the Stripes till he sees Stars." — December 11, 1860.

The passions of the Southern people rose to fever heat and in the South a new confederacy was born. . . . Jeff was to coin a phrase that would boomerang.

IN A POSITION TO BE RECOGNISED.
THE CELEBRATED SEPOY JUGGLER AND ACROBAT, JEFF DAVIS, IN HIS DANGEROUS
GLOBE FEAT

Reports of a plot against his life caused Lincoln to go through Baltimore at night. . . . False tales were spread about this incident and ridicule was heaped upon the President-Elect. . . .

The above Volck etching is founded on the story of Lincoln's flight to Washington wearing a Scotch cap. Lincoln had been persuaded to change his route and time of passing through Baltimore on his way to be inaugurated. It had been learned that the crowd that would gather there would be hostile and probably dangerous, and it was believed that there was a plot to assassinate him. Volck depicts Lincoln fearful of his life, peering out of the partly opened freight door to learn the cause of a horrible noise, only to discover it is nothing more than a frightened cat on top of a hydrant. The car is labeled "Freight — bones; capacity, 000."

THE NEW PRESIDENT OF THE UNITED STATE

FROM A FUGITIVE SKETCH.

Lincoln tried to maintain a peaceful balance.

PROF. LINCOLN IN HIS GREAT FEAT OF BALANCING.

News that Confederate batteries had opened fire on Charleston harbor abruptly ended the long period of uncertainty. . . . Lincoln called for 75,000 volunteers and, as unprepared America moved on to total war, the aged General-In-Chief Winfield Scott planned military death for the Confederate States.

In this cartoon, General Winfield Scott is depicted striking a blow with a cudgel labeled "Liberty and Union" at the Confederate dragon "Secession" with seven heads labeled: "Hatred and Blasphemy" for Toombs; "Lying" for Stephens; "Piracy" for Davis; "Perjury" for Beauregard; "Treason" for Twiggs; "Extortion" for Pickens; and "Robbery" for Floyd.

Scott presented Lincoln with a theory for knocking out the Southerners at one fell swoop through deliberate and relentless military-economic strangulation. This was to be achieved by what the radical press of the North derisively called the Anaconda Plan. Anaconda, by loose definition, means any large snake which crushes its prey. General Scott recommended raising and training additional troops of regulars and volunteers as well as the provision of gun boats and transports for river operations for a powerful movement down the Mississippi to the ocean. By a blockade of the Atlantic and Gulf ports, the ten insurgent states would be completely enveloped in a tight Anaconda squeeze.

GENERAL SCOTT.

THE HERCULES OF THE UNION,

SLAYING THE GREAT DRAGON OF SECESSION.

The Seventh Regiment set forth in style.

A MEMBER OF THE SEVENTH REGIMENT DINING

At Delmonico's,   At Annapolis.

But all the young men were not necessarily eager to don a uniform.

THE VOLUNTARY MANNER IN WHICH SOME OF THE SOUTHERN VOLUNTEERS ENLIST.

It was good news for the Federal forces that spring. "Unconditional Surrender" Grant captured Forts Henry and Donelson, opening the Mississippi River as far as Vicksburg. Farragut, with some aid from Ben Butler, took New Orleans. Political smoke from the flames of the burning Mississippi drifted across the Atlantic, blinding Napoleon and Lord John Russell beyond political recognition of the South. For the time being, anyway.

DESIGN FOR A STATUE OF ENGLISH JUSTICE.

SUGGESTED BY LORD JOHN RUSSELL AND LORD PALMERSTON.

The British Lords, Prime Minister Palmerston and Foreign Minister Russell, are pro-South, but they have to decide which is more important to them, cotton or the freeing of the Negroes in the United States.

But all the young men were not necessarily eager to don a uniform.

THE VOLUNTARY MANNER IN WHICH SOME OF THE SOUTHERN VOLUNTEERS ENLIST.

It was good news for the Federal forces that spring. "Unconditional Surrender" Grant captured Forts Henry and Donelson, opening the Mississippi River as far as Vicksburg. Farragut, with some aid from Ben Butler, took New Orleans. Political smoke from the flames of the burning Mississippi drifted across the Atlantic, blinding Napoleon and Lord John Russell beyond political recognition of the South. For the time being, anyway.

DESIGN FOR A STATUE OF ENGLISH JUSTICE.

SUGGESTED BY LORD JOHN RUSSELL AND LORD PALMERSTON.

The British Lords, Prime Minister Palmerston and Foreign Minister Russell, are pro-South, but they have to decide which is more important to them, cotton or the freeing of the Negroes in the United States.

Blockade runners and Rebel raiders plowed the seas as Lincoln's warships sought to keep John Bull out of the Southern cotton market. . . . Britain's Lord Russell could not decide which way to tip the scales, while Napoleon III seemed ready to make up his mind. . . . Well, almost ready.

A LONG LOOK-OUT.

France.—" Ha ! ha ! my leetle Tom Thumb of a Davis ! Ven you grow so big and can valk all alone, you shall be great friend vith me !"

Federal military success in Missouri followed and Lincoln did a little spring cleaning.

UNCLE SAM giving his Favorite Bull-Terrier "CHARLIE VAN WYCK" a Field-Day
with the CONTRACTORS.

The Army of the Potomac, led by George Brinton McClellan, set out to capture Richmond. . . . some of the men allowed occasional success and frequent imbibations to go to their heads. . . . But the army did not get very far.

In 1863 General McClellan had to appear before the Committee on the Cond of The War to explain his actions or non-actions during the Peninsula Campai The above scene is on one of the gunboats on which he was accused of taki refuge during the campaign. The General's chair is cocked back against the m while he is sipping a drink (mint julep?) through a straw.

In October, General Bishop Leonidas Polk blundered at Perryville.

FANCY SKETCH OF RIGHT REVEREND MAJOR-GENERAL BISHOP POLK HEADING HIS "DIVISION."

At the Battle of Perryville, October 8, 1862, late in the evening, Major General Bishop Leonidas Polk observed Lindell's rebel battery coming into action. Shortly after their arrival, he noticed a body of men he took to be Confederates standing at an angle to this brigade and firing on the newly arrived troops. "Dear me," he said, "this is very sad and must be stopped." He couldn't find any of his young men to send and determined to ride over and settle the matter himself. He cantered up to the officer commanding the regiment that was doing the firing and angrily asked what he meant by shooting his own friends. The man answered in surprise, "I don't think there can be any mistake about it; I am sure they are the enemy."

"Enemy," Polk rejoined, "Why, I have only just left them myself. Cease firing, sir. What is your name?"

"My name is Colonel .... of the .... Indiana. I pray, sir, who are you?"

Polk thus learned to his astonishment that he was in the rear of a regiment of Yankees. He decided to "brazen it out", and, protected by his dark blouse and the increasing darkness, he shook his fist in the Colonel's face, saying:

"I'll show you who I am, sir! Cease firing, sir, at once!"

Whereupon Polk turned his horse and cantered slowly down the line, shouting in an authoritative manner to the Yankees to cease firing. At the same time he experienced a "disagreeable sensation" like "screwing up my back" and calculated how many bullets might hit him between the shoulders at any moment. When he finally managed to reach the Confederate side, he announced to the first Colonel he saw, "Colonel, I have reconnoitered these fellows pretty closely, and there is no mistake who they are; you may get up and go at them."

Colonel Fremantle, the English officer to whom Polk narrated this experience, wrote later that Polk assured him that "the slaughter of that Indiana regiment" was the "greatest" he had ever seen.

Here we see life in the slums of a Northern city as interpreted by Volck. Instead of receiving alms from the well-dressed man, the Negro beggar is handed a tract on slavery. A physician is bargaining with two other Negroes for the purchase of a dead body for dissection.

To the majority of soldiers, their military experience was a new one. Take Mr. Fat-Boy for instance.

MR. FAT-BOY'S MILITARY EXPERIENCE.

Mr. Fat Boy, aged 18, didn't think he would be ordered off, when he joined the "Home Guard."

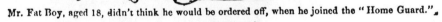

Becomes reconciled, however, when he is made the recipient of many good things.

Somehow he kinder gives out just before the enemy.

But being urged forward by his companions, adopts a new mode of serving his country!

Comes out of the fight, if not wounded, yet showing a very dilapidated condition of clothing.

Is supposed to have done his "duty," from appearances, so is *promoted* and duly glorified!

The draft was always a subject for humor, so was the attitude of the ladies. . . . People still remember the Havelock craze.

GUSHING YOUNG LADY TO DEPARTING ZOUAVE

G. Y. L.—HAVELOCK, SIR ! PRAY, ACCEPT IT.

Zouave:—THANKEE, MISS ; DON'T CARE IF I DO TAKE THAT 'AR LITTLE LOCK OVER YOUR LEFT EAR.—*(Confusion of Gushing Young Lady.)*

Since American women were not familiar with the needs of soldiers at the start of the Civil War, it was inevitable that in the early days their efforts, at times, would be misdirected and blundering. One striking example of such misdirection was the making of Havelocks.

Early in 1861, when the Northern army was moving southward, the soldiers were exposed to unaccustomed heat. A newspaperman recalled that for the British soldiers in India, General Havelock had devised a white linen headdress for the soldiers to wear over their caps to protect them from sunstroke. In his honor the headgear was named the "Havelock." What was good enough for the British was obviously good enough for the boys in Blue and Gray. Army orders were immediately given for the manufacture of Havelocks. Women who were unable to attend Havelock-sewing meetings ordered the material sent to their homes and ran their sewing machines day and night until the headgear was completed. Havelocks were turned out by the thousands both north and south of the Mason-Dixon Line. There was no uniformity about them. All were of different sizes and patterns and of every conceivable material.

The soldiers called the Havelocks "the white nightcaps" and wore them in every possible fashion—as nightcaps, turbans, sunbonnets, bandages and sunshades. The men looked so ludicrous that the fate of the Havelock was sealed. No more time or money was wasted in their manufacture.

THE DRAFT—PLEA FOR EXEMPTION.

CLERK—"*Your age is?*"

EXEMPT—"*My age! Oh, it's exactly sixty-three.*"

CLERK—"*You mean thirty-three.*"

EXEMPT—"*No; sixty-three. I was born the year George Washington died, and remember the circumstance.*"

THE RECRUITING QUESTION.

"*Guess, Judge, I'll resign my locust; all the thieves are in the Rebel army!*"

The people, North and South, discovered that the war was going to last longer than had been anticipated. Death lists lengthened, and there was increased suffering among Southern Civilians. . . .

A new outpouring of cartoons was inspired by events on the battlefront and at home.

LINCOLN'S DREAM; OR, THERE'S A GOOD TIME COMING.

THE LITTLE JOKER.

CHORUS (Greeley, Bennett, Raymond)—"*Know where it is—under that middle hat, of course; under Keyes.*"

THE SITUATION IN OHIO.

LITTLE BUCKEYE. "Daddy, Old Secesh's coming across, sure."
DADDY. "All right, Sonny! but I've ben' waiting a blessed long time for him."

42

On September 22, Abraham Lincoln presented his cabinet with a preview of the Emancipation Proclamation. One Southern artist etched into a cartoon the bitterness of the entire South at this drastic move.

In this carefully-wrought etching, Lincoln is revealed sitting sideways at a table decorated with Negroes' heads with rams' horns, writing his proclamation of freedom. His head is resting on his hand while his left foot is symbolically trampling on the Constitution of the United States which is lying on the floor. The Southerners felt that Lincoln was seeking to destroy the Constitution, for in their eyes, the war and the Proclamation were unconstitutional. On the wall is a picture of the massacres of St. Domingo, the killing of children, and the destruction of homes. A picture of John Brown with a palm in one hand and a pike in the other, and an expression of "cranky benignity" on his face, hangs on the wall. A statue of Liberty is burlesqued with a baboon's head and laurel wreath which it has been said suggests the popular revilement of Lincoln as a gorilla. The devil holds his inkstand, an ass's head is on the back of the chair, and the feet of the table are satanic cloven hoofs. The War, as the Southerners saw it, was nothing more than a fanatical crusade for the Negroes whose ends were to be achieved by the massacre of the white man.

The year 1863 dawned on a period of despair and discouragement for the North. Defeat on the battlefront had helped to foster a lull on the homefront. The flower of the Army of the Potomac had been lost at Fredericksburg. In the West, the Army of the Cumberland was checked in a costly battle at Murfreesboro. Sherman had failed to take Vicksburg, and Richmond was still safe for the Confederacy. Anti-government forces and opponents of the war who had been seeking from the very start to build up a backlog of dissatisfaction for its cause among pro-Union supporters, now seized the opportunity to send out a variety of "peacefeelers."

Congressman Clement L. Vallandigham, leader of the peace-at-any-price Copperhead movement, considerably strengthened his fifth column on January 14, 1863. In a keynote address for the peace group, he delivered his defeatist sentiments to a crowded, attentive House of Representatives.

"Defeat, debt, taxation sepulchres, these are your trophies," he told an audience that had not yet recovered from the bloody defeat at Fredericksburg. "You have not conquered the South. You never will." For an hour and a half he spoke in this fashion and no one interrupted him.

Throughout American history, there have been such outbursts of defeatism by the enemy within. The Revolutionary War had its Tories and "sunshine patriots." In the War of 1812 there were "Blue Light Federalists" who received their name from the type of signaling they did from shore to British ships operating along the New England coast. They refused to support "Mr. Madison's War" and were involved in secession plots. In 1846 there were Abolitionists and Conscience Whigs who urged Mexicans to welcome American soldiers to "hospitable graves."

The Copperheads of the sixties were antiwar Northerners who sympathized strongly with the South, and were willing to settle for any peace terms laid down by the Confederacy. Their ranks were filled with so-called "nigger haters, draft dodgers, embittered editors, and ambitious politicians" who found their strength in Ohio, Indiana, Illinois, Wisconsin, Iowa, and New York. Public figures like the unsavory Wood brothers of New York had tried to cement pro-secession feeling in the North before the outbreak of war, when the conservative businessmen in cities along the Atlantic seaboard were in a responsive mood. While not a Copperhead, Buchanan himself believed disunion was inevitable.

The actual origin of the name Copperhead is uncertain. It was first applied to the pro-Southern Democrats in the July 20, 1861 edition of the *New York Herald,* but long before the Civil War the term was used to describe a person who would strike from concealment without warning. Other terms such as "Tory" and "Butternut," a contemptuous reference to the home-dyed clothing of hillbilly Southern Democrats, did not capture the public imagination as did the name "Copperhead."

The Copperhead badge was the head of Liberty cut from a copper United States cent, and was worn at first as a form of protest against the arbitrary arrests of the government. Cartoonists, however, preferred another symbol for the group and depicted them as loathsome political reptiles. The Leland sketches in particular have an abundance of snakes, many with human heads.

[The following cartoons have been selected from *Ye Book of Copperheads* by C. G.

and E. H. Leland. While their complete meaning is often obscure, the pictures more than any others on the subject tell a fascinating, illuminating story of America's enemy within during the Civil War. The general meaning of a good number of the cartoons and the identity of some of the figures is beyond analysis or explanation. This may have been done deliberately by the artist to protect himself from unpleasant repercussions on the part of the caricatured subjects. If each picture were taken alone, the obscurity of meaning might be a hindrance, but when they are viewed in a group, it is not a detraction.]

A "fifth column" reared its copper head and political reptiles struck across the Northern horizon, hoping for a Confederate victory.

PHILADELPHIA:
FREDERICK LEYPOLDT.
1863.

TITLE-PAGE OF YE BOOK OF COPPERHEADS
ENGRAVED FOR THE COLONIAL SOCIETY OF MASSACHUSETTS FROM A COPY IN THE BOSTON ATHENÆUM

A soldier came back from the war,   with many an honorable scar;
But the Copperheads cried,   "Served you right if you'd died
In this curst *Abolitionist* war!"

"Nor doth this Wood lack Worlds."—Midsummer Night's Dream, II. 2.

There was an old Snake in New York   said for peace all the people should work;
"But if war *must* come,   let us fight here *at home!!*"
Quoth sanguiloquent Ben of New York.

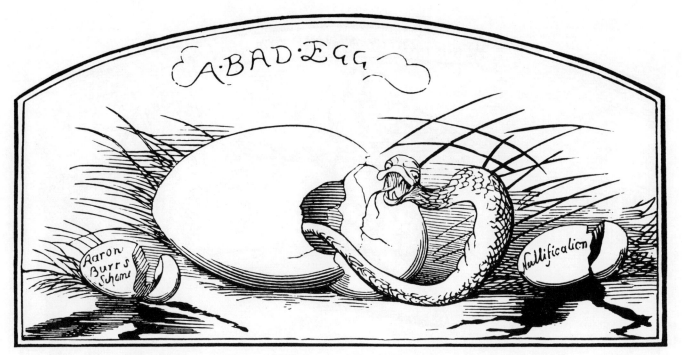

The old Tory dragon is dead,   but she left us some eggs in her stead;
Two were smashed in the yolk,   but the third hatched and broke,
And out came a vile Copperhead.

"And what Stock he springs of!!!"—*Coriolanus*, II. 3.

Copper stocks are uncertain to buy,   though this Copperhead's stock's very high;
But we still might improve   this stock of his love,
By adding the *right* sort of tie.

"Ascend, my CHAMBERS!"—*Merry Wives of Windsor*, III. 3.

There was an old War Horse, a clerical,   who thought our Republic chimerical;
"For the Union," he said,   "he never had prayed,"
This mordacious old War Horse cholerical.

"There is no goodness in the worm."—*Antony and Cleopatra*, V. 2.

The abominable Copperhead worms!   With their wriggles, and twists, and their squirms!
But the gardener, they say,   will soon find out a way
To kill the vile Copperhead worms.

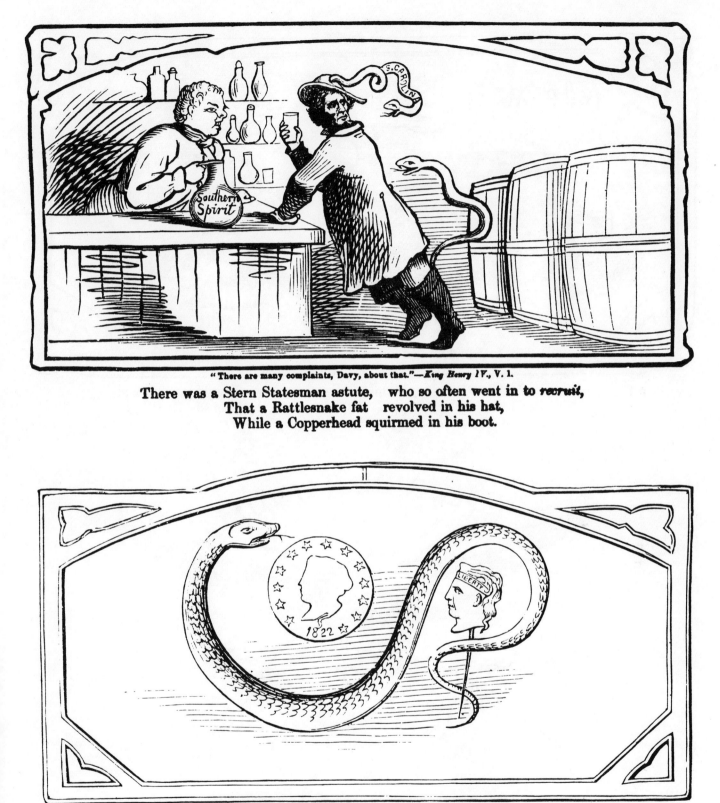

"There are many complaints, Davy, about that."—*King Henry IV.*, V. 1.

There was a Stern Statesman astute,   who so often went in to *recruit*,
That a Rattlesnake fat   revolved in his hat,
While a Copperhead squirmed in his boot.

"So much dishonor my fair stars."—*King Richard III.*, IV. I.

The traitor our Common Cents mars,   And on Liberty plainly he wars,
Taking Freedom away   from the Union, I say,
When he cuts out her head from the stars.

There once was a bottle of PORTER,   which the Copperheads thought was all water;
But when the cork popped,   the Copperheads dropped,
And were stunned by the *vim* of the Porter!

There once was a Snake who said "Hey!   There's an Eagle I'll take for my prey!"
But the bird with his bill   did the Copperhead kill,
And bore him in triumph away.

"Exit shall be strangling a snake."—Love's Labor's Lost, V. 1.

The Copperhead traitors all, our army "base hirelings" call !
But some fine summer day The "boys," just for play,
Will settle the Copperheads all.
AMEN !

Discouragement in the North began to melt away with the winter snows. Everywhere there was evidence of new hope of victory. Union rallies were held and the case for the Emancipation Proclamation was presented. Warnings were issued that for every conspiring Copperhead, there was a tree or lamppost from which he could be hanged. The indignation on the part of the soldiers at the battlefront toward the Copperheads and those who wanted to make a peace with the South heartened the war supporters at home. As early as February 19, 1863, seventy-five convalescent soldiers from a hospital near Keokuk, Iowa, went out in mid-afternoon, entered the office of the pro-Copperhead *Keokuk Constitution,* wrecked the presses, dumped the type out the window, and created general havoc. Many military men threatened retribution on their return home.

By the summer of 1864 there was dwindling confidence in the outcome of the war. Even Lincoln himself took a dim view of the political outlook and was certain the Democratic party would come into power in the November presidential elections. The Union military seemed to be bogged down on all fronts. The siege of Petersburg had become an indeterminate stalemate. The financial condition of the country was unstable. Paper currency fell in value to one-third of that of gold. From the Republican viewpoint, it was an unpropitious moment for the President to issue a call for 500,000 additional volunteers. The draft was unpopular and public response apathetic. Many, influenced by the emboldened peace leaders, favored the abandonment of the war. Copperhead propaganda had inflamed the mobs in the New York draft riots of 1863. There was no reason why it couldn't succeed again. Brazenly, the Copperhead congressmen on the floor of the House clamored for a change of rulers, a peaceful settlement of the war, and recognition of the independence of the Southern states. Men had been imprisoned for making less treasonable statements. But this scene on Capitol Hill was but a preview of the treasonous drama that was to be enacted at the Democratic convention later that summer.

The Democrats were committed to an unconditional peace platform and, for a time, it looked as though Clement Vallandigham of Ohio would head a peace ticket. But both war and peace factions had to be appeased to ensure unanimity at the convention and victory at the polls. Governor Horatio Seymour of New York and the majority of delegates from the East felt that a peace program would be fatal to the Northeast. At the same time there was a danger that Ohio and other midwestern states might bolt the party if their demands were overlooked. Party bosses sat at the bargaining table with financiers and hopeful politicians and hatched a compromise.

On Monday, August 29, the Democratic National Convention assembled in the wigwam at Chicago where four years earlier the Republicans had nominated Abraham Lincoln for the presidency. The tone and spirit of the convention has been likened to that of the antidraft riots in New York in July, 1863. The Federal government was shamefully vilified. The key plank of the platform presented was the second resolution, which stated in part:

That this convention does explicitly declare as the sense of the American people, that after four years of failure to restore the Union by the experiment of War, . . . justice, humanity, liberty and the public welfare demand that immediate efforts be made for a cessation of hostilities, with a view to an ultimate convention of the States, or other peaceable means, to the end that at the earliest practicable moment peace may be restored, on the basis of the Federal Union of the States.

This resolution was a triumph for Vallandigham, who was the hero of the convention. The Peace Democrats had captured the platform, but a political bargain had been made. Something had been promised the War Democrats in return, and that something was the nomination of the young and dashing Major General George Brinton McClellan. McClellan received the nomination on the first ballot, whereupon Vallandigham moved that the nomination be made unanimous. There was compensation for the Peace party in the nomination of one of their number, George H. Pendleton, of Ohio, for Vice-President.

Because of his military upbringing and predilection for continuing the war, McClellan could not countenance any surrender. In his September 8 answer to the Democratic Committee of Notification, he concluded: "The Union must be preserved at all hazards." This letter of guarantee from a soldier that the Union would not be abandoned still left war as well as peace as possible means for preserving the Union. It disgusted his Democratic adversaries and evoked a storm of criticism from those who had voted for him; they now labeled him "worse than Lincoln." It began to look as though the little general who had been too slow to make a decision on the battlefield had been too quick in making one in the political arena.

On December 21, 1864, in his final call for troops, Lincoln sought 300,000 volunteers. Deficiencies were to be met by conscription on February 15. Despite approaching victory, the response was slow, particularly in the midwest. Surprisingly few men were interested in taking part in the final moment of triumph, but rather sought new ways to avoid the draft. Even in those days, there were skillful "operators." False certificates of service or physical incapacity were the fashion of the hour. Provost marshals permitted draft associations to furnish substitutes in proportion to their numbers on special arrangement, and bounty jumpers appeared to be making new records. Local boards sought to enlist runaway Southern Negroes, Confederate prisoners, and even convicts.

On May 10, 1865, when Jefferson Davis was captured at Irwinsville, Georgia, by the 4th Michigan Cavalry, it was the occasion for great jubilation. The word was that he had run away disguised as a woman. It seemed a likely act of cowardice on the part of the man who had been part of a great rebellion and led his people to defeat. There was probably no more basis of truth to this cruel rumor than to the one about Lincoln's passage through Baltimore as a Scot. In the Confederate Museum in Richmond there is a letter from the Union officer who captured Davis, testifying that he was in full uniform at the time, with a shawl across his shoulders—a quite common garb among men of that period. Nevertheless, dozens of cartoons were circulated featuring Davis in bonnet and skirt; some even appeared on the title pages of sheet music.

Southern cartoonists did not depict much cheer in the North at the beginning of 1864. A popular theme for their cartoons was the eagerness on the part of the freed Negroes to return to rebeldom to escape cruel Northerners—Ben Butler in particular.

THE RETURNED PRODIGAL.

DINAH.—Great sakes alive! Cum back from de Yankees?

SAMBO.—Yes, mighty glad to git back to marster. De Ole Boy down to Norfolk, he call heself Butler, but I knows dat he cum from below. One eye looks up to Hebben as if he is watchin what is doin up dare; tother eye looks down to de pocket, watchin what's dare. He is monstrous hard on black folks. It was work, work, all de time, and so I runs away and cums home.

As soldiers on the battlefront raised their voices against the "peace snakes," the morale of the people rose. Newspapers began to scotch the snake. . . .

THE COPPERHEAD PLAN FOR SUBJUGATING THE SOUTH.

War and Argument—Cold Steel and Cool Reason—having failed to restore the Union, it is supposed that the South may be *bored* into coming back.

Our Picture represents the successful operation of this exceedingly humane and ingenious device.

This cartoon was executed by Frank H. T. Bellew for Harper's. It depicts several prominent pacifists standing before a man representing the Confederacy who is stretching and yawning. They implore him to come back and he says, "Oh! dear, I can't stand this much longer." The legend reads: "War and Argument — Cold Steel and Cool Reason — having failed to restore the Union, it is supposed that the South may be BORED into coming back."

In March Ulysses Grant was commissioned lieutenant general and placed in supreme command of the Union Armies. He assigned control of action in the West to General William T. Sherman, and the two commanders oiled their war machines for an advance on the Confederacy. Activities of the peace movements faded temporarily from the limelight. John Bull and Napoleon wanted no truck with the Confederacy now. . . . And the South suspected Lincoln of making a deal with England.

The Yankee-British Alliance against France!

OLD ABE.—Come Johnny, Don't be afraid. Give me your hand; I thought it would be a *good joke* to scare you a little; but I don't intend to hurt you, so let us be friends, and keep our eyes upon Monsieur Louis, I tell you he's tricky

JOHN BULL.—Now, Habe, you don't treat me right. Hi want to be neutral, you know, that's all. Hi don't know but Old Jeff may whip you yet, and Hi must look out for my hinterests, you know. If Louis goes to playing any tricks on me, by George I'll play the devil with his Maximilian.

In the early fall, the military tide turned. On September 2, Atlanta fell to Sherman. On September 19, Phil Sheridan won the Third Battle of Winchester, the first of a series of great battles which drove the Confederates from the Shenandoah Valley. . . . There was great devastation in the tracks of the armies.

Naughty Little Phil.

SHERMAN'S MARCH THROUGH GEORGIA.

OPINIONS OF RICHMOND PAPERS, ILLUSTRATED.

WHAT THE CONFEDERATE GENERALS DID.—It is said that Beauregard, Hood, Forrest and Wheeler danced for joy when they heard that Sherman had cut loose from Atlanta.—*Richmond Enquirer.*

WHAT THE RICHMOND EDITORS DID—Let the editors of the Richmond papers meet and compare notes. If we are firm and spirited, Sherman can't hurt us.—*Richmond Sentinel.*

STARVING SHERMAN'S ARMY.—Thank God, not a pound of meat of any kind will be found in Sherman's course through Georgia.—*Richmond Whig.*

HOW THE YANKEES WERE HARASSED.—We understand, from reliable sources, that the Yankees have not enjoyed a moment's rest since they left Atlanta.—*Richmond Star.*

HOW SHERMAN'S ARMY WAS RECEIVED.—As the Yankees march through the towns, they are received in sullen silence by all classes.—*Richmond Enquirer.*

HOW THE YANKEES ENTERED SAVANNAH.—Savannah has fallen! The vandals had the impudence to enter Savannah mounted on cattle which they had stolen from Georgia farmers. But the invaders can never take Charleston.—*Richmond Sentinel.*

Union Republicans decided not to change horses in midstream, and nominated Lincoln for a second term in the White House.

As the public suffered a delayed reaction to the spring military reverses, anti-war factions mustered their forces. The Copperheads decided it was a good time to strike and the Democratic convention proved to be the proper place.

A compromise had to be made to keep all factions happy and the former idol of the Army of the Potomac curled up beside a Copperhead.

As the public suffered a delayed reaction to the spring military reverses, anti-war factions mustered their forces. The Copperheads decided it was a good time to strike and the Democratic convention proved to be the proper place.

A compromise had to be made to keep all factions happy and the former idol of the Army of the Potomac curled up beside a Copperhead.

. . . and proceeded to attempt a double feat which made him the favorite butt as well as the favorite candidate on the graphic scene.

In this unsigned lithographic cartoon, General McClellan, Presidential aspirant on the Democratic Party ticket, stands in the center of a circus ring, depicted as an acrobatic horseman trying to ride two horses pulling in opposite directions. They are labeled "Letter of Acceptance" and "Chicago Platform," and Pendleton, Vice-Presidential candidate for the Democratic Party, is a clown at the ringside, crying: "I say, Mac! can't you hold on to BOTH 'till the 8th of Nov.?" Outlines of hats in the background suggest a large audience. To the left a band is playing and a big drum labeled "N.Y. World" is prominently displayed.

To RICHMOND 10 MILES.

THE "IF" CANDID.

"If he had not been interfered with."—IF THE DOG

"Your *if* is the *only* Peace-Maker; much virtue in *if*."

TE forthe PRESIDENCY.

d not stopped, he would have caught the FOX!!!

General Touchstone, in as you like it, act. V, sc. IV.

ACROBATIC NOVELTIES.

A DIFFICULT TRICK (WALKING ON A LONG AND A SHORT STILT) NOW IN REHEARSAL BY PROFESSOR GEORGE B. M'CLELLAN. ALSO THE ONE STILT PERFORMANCE OF THE EXPERT PENDLETON.

A humorous presentation of the Democratic situation in 1864 again depicts acrobat George B. McClellan in a circus ring. McClellan is trying to walk on uneven stilts which pull him in opposite directions. They are labeled "War" and "Peace"— "Peace" is almost buried in the ground. George Hunt Pendleton, candidate for Vice-President, is standing with one foot on a stilt, trying obviously to hold his position until the forthcoming election. The cartoon points out the discrepancy of the Peace Plank in the Chicago Platform of the Democratic Party. The Peace Plank had been violently attacked by many who felt that the Southerners were beaten and no favorable terms should be extended to them. Now, just a few days before the election, McClellan is still trying to strike a balance.

66

THE WAR CANDIDATE ON A PEACE PLATFORM.

Harper's Weekly offered the Copperheads a new plan. . . . And two Nast cartoons helped
to arouse the North and gain votes for Lincoln and Johnson.

These two cartoons are said to have done more for the Union cause than any hitherto published. They stirred the public and gained new supporters for the Republican ticket. COMPROMISE WITH THE SOUTH, the first, represented the defiant Southerner clasping hands with the crippled Northern soldier over the grave of Union heroes who had died in a useless war. Columbia is bowed in sorrow and in the background a Negro family is pictured enchained once more.

This cartoon proved to be such a success that an increased edition of Harper's Weekly had to be printed to meet the demand, and the plate was used for a campaign.

WITH THE SOUTH

GUERRILLA WARFARE
BARBARITIES
FORT PILLOW
LAWRENCE
STARVING YANKEE PRISONERS
NO QUARTER
BURNING CHAMBERSBURG
YANKEE KILLERS MINN
MURDERERS
BAYONETING THE WOUNDED
SCALPING

CSA

SOUTH

ITION.

THE CHICA

As Election Day, 1864, approached, there was anxiety about New York City where the draft riots had taken place a year earlier. According to Butler himself, it was feared that "without the restraining presence of a resolute soldier, backed by an imposing military force, a lawless mob would take possession of the ballot boxes and the city." Benjamin Butler was finally designated as the resolute soldier to keep the peace in New York City.

According to this cartoonist, other means were resorted to for safeguarding the ballot boxes for Lincoln.

Lithograph by J. E. Baker. An armed Negro keeps maimed soldier from voting for McClellan. One poll clerk tells another to pretend to see nothing.

Northern leaders faced the familiar problem of attracting new recruits . . . uniforms added glamor to a military ball . . . dodging the draft was a popular sport which the ladies tried to discourage.

*Arabella, (who adores the defenders of our Union.)—*Oh! Augustus, how eloquently Col. De Shann describes the action at Bull-Run, and with what modesty he speaks of himself on that occasion. Oh, how I *do* wish you were a major—or captain—or—or something 'nice.'"

THE BEST KIND OF RECRUITING SERGEANT.

Re-Cook.—"Give us a kiss, Mary?"
Parlor Maid.—"Don't bother me! Why ain't you away soldiering with the rest you great hulking fellow?—Kisses is for them that comes back!"

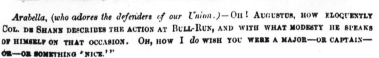

THE ART OF INSPIRING COURAGE.

HOW FATHERS MAY IMPEL THEIR SONS TO DEEDS OF VALOR.
"Want money, sir?—come to me for money? Look there, sir!"

SECOND METHOD, NOT SO ECONOMICAL.
"Here, my son, is your commission *as Colonel—cost me five thousand dollars, sir!"*

As the year 1865 dawned on wartorn America, with the continuing victories of Northern armies, peace advocates were refused military passes to the South.

Petersburg fell and Richmond was in flames. Success—and spirits went to the head of many a man.

Defeat knocked on the door of the White House of the Confederacy, while, inside, the master of the house was "calmly contemplating."

JEFF DAVIS "CALMLY CONTEMPLATING."

"Our country is now environed with perils which it is our duty calmly to contemplate."— *Extract from Davis's last Message.*

And then the holocaust ended. Lee surrendered at Appomattox. The time was close at hand for Johnny to come marching home. But there was no glory. Just weariness and heartbreak and a knowledge that the real job still lay ahead. The job of making one nation indivisible with liberty and justice for all. . . . But before the North could savor the taste of victory, the greatest tragedy of all befell the nation. The man the people called the Great Emancipator, the humanitarian, the leader who had borne his country's burdens for four long years, fell at the hands of a fanatical actor. . . . The nation mourned. But life had to go on. The President is dead; long live the President. Andrew Johnson moved into the White House. Postwar business had to be dealt with. No time now for tears. It was going to be a time for revenge. Get the leaders. Get the rebels who started the whole thing. No one stopped to ask what? how? or why? . . . Jefferson Davis was one. Hang Jeff Davis on the sour apple tree. Hang. Kill. Get revenge . . . funny? Not really, but some situations inevitably lend themselves to graphic humor. Rumor had it that the former President of the Confederacy fled from Richmond wearing female attire. This was a natural for the caricaturist's pencil, and he drew every ounce of humor possible from the episode.

Published at III

"Don't provoke the Preside

THE CAPTURE O

His last official act "The ad

He attempts to "Clear his Skir

In **THE CAPTURE OF JEFF DAVIS**, Davis is shown running, holding up skirts over his trousers with one hand and a raised dagger in the other. He is pursued by a cavalry officer on horseback, with soldiers following in the rear. A lone horse precedes Davis with a bag hanging on its saddle. It reads: "Confederate Gold." This lithograph was published shortly after his capture.

...av. St N.Y. (up stairs.)

...r he may hurt some of you!"

JEFF DAVIS.

...on of a new rebel uniform."

...ut finds it "All up in Dixie".

The original engraved cartoon entitled **THE HEAD OF THE CONFEDERACY** depicts Davis in a woman's dress, struggling on the ground with a pistol in one hand and a dagger in the other. An officer stands in front of him with a raised sword and pointed pistol. Another soldier has hold of Davis' skirt in the rear, exposing his trousers and boots. Mrs. Davis speaks: "Don't provoke the President or some of you might get hurt! !"

THE HEAD OF THE CONF

JERACY ON A NEW BASE.

THE WAY IN WHICH JEFF. DAVIS LEFT RICHMOND.—LINE OF MARCH—STRAIGHT OUT OF THE CITY.

1. Cavalry.

3. Civil Authorities.

2. Infantry.

4. Firemen.

5. Trades.

6. The crowd.

This cartoon appeared on the title page of Sheet Music, "Jeff in Petticoats: A So **for the Times," by George Cooper. Musical composition by Henry Tucker. T** **cartoon was lithographed by H. C. in New York.**

II

Cartoons Abroad

Although no foreign nations participated in the great American War of the sixties, several did contemplate intervention quite seriously until it became obvious that the North had the situation well in hand.

The attitude of France and England in particular was sharply emphasized in contemporary cartoons. Patronizing John Bull and vacillating Louis Napoleon were held up to ridicule in London, Paris, and American papers.

The British had not wanted to see civil war in the United States, for they feared it would "interfere with the commercial world of which they were the center" and halt business relations between the two countries. The *New York Herald,* however, charged that abolitionism was a devilish contrivance of the British ruling classes to break down American institutions. The *New York Times* was certain that Americans were aware of the base selfishness and "canting hypocrisy" of the British governing classes, while the *New York World* felt that the French could judge the American situation more objectively because they were less involved than the British.

When fighting did break out in South Carolina, the British upper classes immediately revealed their pro-Southern leanings. Apathy toward the North increased throughout England, although the issue of slavery prevented a complete swing toward the Confederacy. The English, for the most part, were opposed to having slaveholders as allies. The clergy was anti-war, but very few sympathized with the Union. Bishop Samuel Wilberforce wanted to see the South recognized. *Punch* ridiculed the North after First Bull Run for continuing the war, while at the same time calling the Confederacy a "kettle as black as a pot." *Punch* spoke of the contrast between the United States and Italy, suggesting that Columbia would soon have to hand over to Italy her motto *E Pluribus Unum*. Gladstone, Chancellor of the Exchequer, considered separation of the States unavoidable. Lord John

Russell, head of the foreign office, was known to refer to "the late Union." Besides all this, the British needed cotton and they objected to the Northern blockade of Southern waters.

At the very outset of the war, the Confederacy had no navy. They scouted through every Southern port for merchant steamers that could be bought or seized, and then armed and commissioned in the Confederate Navy. Captain Raphael Semmes, who became a one-man menace to Federal shipping, was given the packet *Habana*, renamed the *Sumter*, which had plied between Cuba and New Orleans, and he remained on excellent terms with foreign powers, particularly the French throughout the War. But the ships thus taken over were not enough for the Confederate navy. Britain's shipbuilders came to the rescue.

Shortly after the *Sumter* was commissioned, James Bulloch, secret naval agent extraordinary of the C.S.A., succeeded in getting a contract for the construction of merchant ships first with Miller and Sons, shipbuilders at Liverpool, and then with Laird Brothers, the largest shipbuilding firm in England. The British government would not fit out armed ships for either belligerent, but it said nothing about merchantmen built in Britain and armed on the high seas. These ships drastically depleted the United States Merchant Marine, and Charles Francis Adams, Union Minister to Britain protested sharply against Britain's ill-disguised aid to the Southern states. Bulloch himself was certain that it would not be too long before Britain might enforce stricter application of the Foreign Enlistment Act which forbade British subjects to enlist within the realm on vessels belonging to either one of the belligerent forces.

On November 8, 1861, the British mail packet *Trent* was leaving Havana, Cuba, with two Confederate Commissioners on board, Senators James Mason and John Slidell. They were en route to Britain and France under the protection of the British flag to seek recognition of the Confederacy. Captain Charles Wilkes of the Federal war steamer *San Jacinto* sighted the *Trent* and, over the protest of her captain, triumphantly removed the two commissioners and brought them to the United States shores as prisoners. The British were outraged. Many believed war between England and the North was imminent. Lincoln thought it the lesser of two evils to release Mason and Slidell. Americans abroad likewise sought to pacify the British Lion. Other forces stepped in and soon the excitement died down.

After Lincoln issued his Emancipation Proclamation, many religious groups in France and England changed their attitudes. The London Emancipation Society, which issued pro-Union pamphlets, was formed.

Had England recognized the Confederacy, it is quite possible, in the opinion of many historians, that Louis Napoleon would have followed suit. For Napoleon was eager to wage war on the United States although he professed to be neutral. The exploits of Captain Semmes on the seas thrilled the French, and Parisian newspapers compared him to John Paul Jones. In fact, at one point the French were engaged in building ironclad rams for the Confederacy to be used in breaking the Northern blockade.

In 1863 the Confederacy was in dire need of credit. Its embargo on the export of cotton had failed to produce an effective cotton shortage in the European textile industry because both Egypt and India were able to furnish new supplies. The Paris banking house of Erlanger and Company floated a loan which was secured by cotton held by the Confederacy. It was issued in Paris, London, Liverpool, Frankfurt, and Amsterdam. Subscriptions were closed in two days. Fifteen million dollars was subscribed in London. The Confederates tried to play up the initial success of the loan and present it as a serious investment. Others, however, looked upon it as pure speculation. The chief advantage of the loan, according to one historian, is the fact that "it made the average layman feel that the Southern cause was respectable."

The Union Treasury did not seek financing from abroad. After a time a number of United States bonds were bought in Europe. American dollars were very cheap and would prove extremely profitable as an investment in the event of a Northern victory.

Spain would have been very pleased had England recognized the Confederacy, as she would not have been obliged to proclaim her neutrality. The Spanish upper classes despised the Yankees and blamed the United States government for filibustering* in Cuba, their "Pearl of the Antilles." They were certain that the Confederates would prove to be their friends.

At the outset of the war, Russia, cooperating with Britain and France, had granted Confederate merchantmen a status similar to that of the merchant ships of the kingdom of Italy, still not recognized. But to keep the United States in power as a "counterpoise" to England, Alexander II himself told the American Minister in 1861 that he sympathized with the cause of Emancipation. He had freed the Russian serfs that same year.

Late in 1863 it looked as though the Czar had decided to take sides in the American War after all, when two units of the Imperial Navy sailed into the New York and San Francisco harbors bearing messages of good will. Society wined and dined the officers and a civic dinner was held at the Astor House for the Russian admiral and crew. The supposedly friendly gesture came at a time when the North welcomed any friendly hand except an empty one. The past summer had witnessed the bloody draft riots in cities throughout the North, and there had been organized demands for peace. It turned out later that Russia was having her hands full trying to suppress a revolt in Poland and, fearing that the British and French might attempt military intervention and blockade her navy there, she had sought the security of American harbors.

In Italy, Garibaldi was completely on the side of the North and even considered going to America to take over a military command under the Federal government.

The London Emancipation Society, which had from the start issued pro-Union pamphlets, showed itself partisan to the Union cause when it persuaded Henry Ward Beecher to make a lecture tour through England. Beecher, a dynamic preacher with a magnetic personality, arrived in the British Isles in October and delivered his talks in the largest towns of the kingdom. Large crowds came to hear him—hecklers as well as supporters.

The meeting at Exeter Hall October 20, 1863, attracted the greatest attention. Not all of the ten thousand people present were Beecher supporters, but the Yankee preacher was at his best when handling hecklers and large audiences.

The upper-class press considered the meeting "absurd, a burlesque, an affair of hired claquers." The *Weekly Dispatch* referred to the London and Manchester Federal sympathizers as "canting pulpiteers! Those medicine men and rainmakers of this pagan Christiandom! Your Newmans and Beechers, and Noels and Cheevers and mouthing Massies. . . ." All, according to this paper, were for more slaughters. The *Daily News* insisted that

*Irregular military adventuring.

the Exeter Hall demonstration was representative of the people, "even though not of the Church of England and the nobility." *Punch* accused Beecher of feeding treacle (British for molasses), to the British Lion. Despite the criticism, the demonstrations in favor of Beecher were too hearty to please the Confederacy. Jefferson Davis found no consolation in news of the poorly attended pro-Southern meetings in London. It was quite obvious that the British were losing confidence in the future of the South.

Enthusiasm for the Confederacy had continued to dwindle as military success for the North took an upswing. Louis Napoleon had not ceased trying to unite Europe into recognition of the South, for he was faced with great unemployment at home and was in desperate need of cotton to keep the French textile mills going. However, at this stage Napoleon himself was quite busy, even if his spindles weren't. He had availed himself of the opportunity of taking control of Mexico while Uncle Sam's back was turned, and had placed the hapless Archduke Maximilian on the Mexican throne. Meanwhile, his agent was seeking —behind closed doors, of course—to detach Texas from the Confederacy.

Sentiment in England was shifting more and more toward the North. Although the people were still divided in their opinion on Lincoln's Emancipation Proclamation, a great many began to look upon it with favor. Religious societies gradually modified their anti-Union attitudes and the British press, too, became more conciliatory.

Part of this change in attitude can be attributed to the fact that, because of their military victories, the administration in Washington was able to take a stronger stand with England and Europe. They could even do a little threatening of their own, for they were determined to put an end to British shipbuilding for the Confederacy. The Northern navy had grown in size and power, and Congress had passed a law authorizing privateers. Britain well knew what some of the consequences might be if American privateers were turned loose on Britain's scattered merchant fleet. Napoleon, too, was not unaware of this danger.

To intervene or not to intervene; that was the great question facing the Old World powers in the early days of the American Civil War. . . . The British and French didn't cotton to the blockade any more than did the Confederacy.

Others never seemed quite sure what the struggle was all about.

While shilly-shallying Louis Napoleon continued to wait for John Bull to genuflect before King Cotton, Abe Lincoln pulled out his first plum with the capture of New Orleans. John Bull and his pal across the channel were both impressed. . . . But not for long. . . . Too many reverses.

In the first place, Lincoln had let George do it and he didn't.

And in the second place, Gladstone wanted a bull market, not a Bull Run. . . . It was a field day for the foreign cartoonists. . . . They tendered a bit of advice to Columbia.

NAUGHTY JONATHAN.

THE WILFUL BOY.

Jonathan. "I WILL FIGHT—I WILL HAVE A **NATIONAL DEBT** LIKE OTHER PEOPLE!"

KING COTTON BOUND;

Or, The Modern Prometheus.

The poem that accompanies this cartoon commences: "Far across Atlantic waters Groans in chains a giant king . . ." The cartoon depicts "King Cotton bound; or, The Modern Prometheus." King Cotton is bound by chains — the Blockade. The Eagle, with both Southern and Northern stars, is tearing out his vitals.

INDIAN COTTON DEPÔT

COTTON STORES

OVER THE WAY.

Mr. Bull. "OH! IF YOU TWO LIKE FIGHTING BETTER THAN BUSINESS, I SHALL DEAL AT **THE OTHER SHOP.**"

The poem that accompanies this cartoon begins:
"Cousin Jonathan, listen, and don't
make a row,
Nor fancy you'll see the British lion afraid,
We beg to inform you we've taken a vow,
On the earliest occasion to break your blockade."

In this cartoon, India bows to John Bull, who turns away from South and North fighting in the doorway.

Mr. Bull: "Oh! If you two like fighting better than business, I shall deal at the other shop."

Cartoonists abroad presented a variety of opinions on the American Civil War. Some could not see any difference between Johnny Reb and Billy Yank.

THE AMERICA

JUGGERNAUT.

This cartoon is another example of the lack of distinction between the armies in the eyes of the Europeans and English.

John Bull had been certain the Americans would not fight a war. . . . One French cartoonist seemed convinced the Americans did not know how to fight a war.

LE NORD. Excusez-moi si je ne vous donne pas un coup de sabre : j'ai la grippe.
LE SUD. Cela tombe bien ! je n'aurais pas pu vous le rendre : j'ai la grippe aussi.

Derniere victoire ! Les fédéraux battant la semelle.

These are two small cartoons from L'Illustration.

    1. North: "Pardon me if I don't run you through with my sword; I have the grippe."

    South: "Good thing. I shouldn't be able to knock you out either; I have the grippe too."

    2. Last Victory! The Federals dance a jig.

THE NEW ORLEANS PLUM.

BIG LINCOLN HORNER,
UP IN A CORNER,
THINKING OF HUMBLE PIE;

FOUND UNDER HIS THUMB,
A NEW ORLEANS PLUM,
AND SAID, WHAT A 'CUTE YANKEE AM I!

THE NEW ORLEANS PLUM

Big Lincoln Horner,
Up in a corner,
Thinking of humble pie;
Found under his thumb,
A New Orleans Plum,
And said, "What a cute Yankee am I!"

In the picture, Lincoln is seated in front of map, the name New Orleans after Corinth and Bull Run. The Union army had been defeated at First Bull Run July 21, 1861, Farragut captured New Orleans April 28, 1862, and Halleck took Corinth May 30, 1862.

THE "SENSATION" STRUGGLE IN AMERICA.

The "Sensation" struggle in America. North and South battle on the brink of bankruptcy chasm.

THE LATEST FROM AMERICA;

Or, the New York "Eye-Duster," to be taken Every Day.

THE LATEST FROM AMERICA; or, the New York "Eye-Duster," to be taken Every Day.

Lincoln pours from "victory" goblet into "defeat."

The Tories stigmatized Lincoln's Emancipation Proclamation in advance as his "last card."

ABE LINCOLN'S LAST CARD; OR, ROUGE-ET-NOIR.

This phrase was used as early as December 14, 1861, by the Times of London in speculation on the results of Charles Sumner's agitations for emancipation. In the fall of 1862, Lincoln's preliminary Emancipation Proclamation was published for the perusal of the nation and the world. The South was enraged. In England the Tories stigmatized the document as a "deadly instrument of vengeance on the South," and called it Lincoln's "last card." It could have been more properly labeled his trump card. The phrase caught the fancy of the lesser papers and was taken up by them. The great fear on the part of the Tories was that the Proclamation would arouse public opinion in France and England against their taking an active part in the American War.

But for the liberal elements abroad, it proved a trump card. Despite improvement in the political scene, sympathy for the North remained dormant there until Henry Ward Beecher whistlestopped through England.

" BEECHER'S AMERICAN SOOTHING SYRUP."

A great demonstration greeted his appearance at Exeter Hall. Mr. Punch wrote his own poem about the Reverend Mr. Beecher.

LAIRDS
YARD

BRITISH PLUCK.

This cartoon is from Comic News an English magazine which is not well known and was of short duration. It refers to the building of ships for the Confederacy by the Laird Brothers in Liverpool.

Lincoln, licensed drover, stands before the small Russell. Both are in front of Laird's Yard. Lincoln has a threatening attitude.

Lincoln: "Now, drover boy Jack, if you let out them rams, I won't answer for the consequences."

Russell: (very humbly) "No, sir — please sir — I'll do whatever you tells me, sir — in course, Sir — yes, Sir — please, Sir."

In June of 1864, Captain Raphael Semmes, C.S.N., and his crew on the Alabama were in need of rest. They entered the French harbor of Cherbourg on the English Channel. There the Federal sloop of war Kearsarge engaged the Alabama in battle, and the Kearsarge was sunk. That was the end of Semmes' career as a Rebel sea raider whom the French likened to John Paul Jones.

Le capitaine confédéré Semmes ayant la gracieuseté d'attendre l'arrivee du train de plaisir parti de Paris pour commencer le branle-bas de combat.

In this cartoon, Semmes is standing on the bow of his ship. The translated French caption reads: "The Confederate Captain Semmes having the graciousness to await the arrival of the pleasure train which has left from Paris in order to commence the branle-bas (clearing the decks) of battle."

The British lion prepared to lie down beside the Union eagle, even though John Bull could not help being a little critical. . . . Napoleon was ready to abandon the Confederacy. . . . Captain Semmes of the C.S.N. tried to woo the Emperor back to his first love, but Napoleon was suffering from a touch of Mal de rebel mer.

1863

1864

COLUMBIA'S SEWING-MACHINE.

Mʳ· Britannia. "AH, MY DEAR COLUMBIA, IT'S ALL VERY WELL;
BUT I'M AFRAID YOU'LL FIND IT DIFFICULT TO JOIN *THAT* NEATLY."

106

On the death of Abraham Lincoln, Britannia offered Columbia condolences.

BRITANNIA SYMPATHISES WITH COLUMBIA.

III
Lyrical Laughs

Vanity Fair considered Abolitionists enemies of the Union. The magazine attacked repeatedly such people as Wendell Phillips, Horace Greeley, and Henry Ward Beecher for being of that group. A parody of "Abou Ben Adhem" (entitled "Abo Bo Lition"), read:

Abo Bo Lition (may his tribe decrease!)
Awoke one night not very well at ease,
And saw within the shadow of his room,
Making it mean, and like a stink-weed in bloom,
A devil writing in a book of brass:
Exceeding cant had made *Bo Lition* an ass
And to the shadow he said, a little pale,
"What scribblest thou?" The Phantom raised its tail
And answered with a leer of sour discord.
"The names of those who own *Jeff Davis* Lord."
"And is mine one?" said *Abo*. "Not quite so,"
Replied the devil. *Abo* spoke more low
But cheerly still, aching to grasp his pen,
"Write me as one who hates the Union then."
The devil wrote and vamosed. The next night
He came again—this time a little tight—
And showed the names who served *Jeff Davis* best,
And lo! *Bo Lition's* name led all the rest.

When Major Anderson stole from Fort Moultrie to Fort Sumter in Charleston Harbor with his men, he caused a nationwide commotion, and "urchins in Northern streets cheered him with a bouncy rhyme."

> Bob Anderson, my beau, Bob
> when we were first aquent,
> You were in Mex-i-co, Bob
> because by order sent;
> But now you are in Sumter, Bob
> because you chose to go,
> And blessings on you anyhow, Bob
> Anderson, my beau.[1]

Shortly before Lincoln's inaugural, Major Robert Anderson was at Fort Sumter awaiting reinforcements. General Pickens was in Charleston, hoping Major Anderson would go. And, of course, President James Buchanan was counting the days to his release from the White House. The South couldn't resist taking a final "poke" at old Buck and launching a new one at the government-elect.

> James is in his Cabinet
> Doubting and debating
> Anderson's in Sumter,
> Very tired of waiting.
>
> Pickens is in Charleston
> Blustering of blows;
> Thank goodness March
> The Fourth is near,
> To nip Secession's nose.[2]
>
> Now glory be to Uncle Abe;
> And Scott, his bully pet,
> And Seward, cook and bottle-
> Washer of the Cabinet,
> And glory to the mighty fleet,
> That stood off Charleston Bar,
> And left the dauntless Anderson
> To bear the brunt of War![3]

Thankful to men like Beauregard, the people of the South were filled with optimism in the summer of 1861. They could even write a parody of First Manassas (Bull Run):

> At Bull Run where the sun was low,
> Each Southern face grew pale as snow,
> While loud as jackdaws rose the crow
> Of Yankees boasting terribly!

1 *Harper's Weekly,* January 26, 1861.
2 Frank Moore (ed.) , *The Rebellion Record,* Vol. 1, p. 23.
3 Ibid. p. 92, quoted from *Charleston Mercury.*

But Bull Run saw another sight,
When at the deepening shades of night,
Towards Fairfax Court-house rose the flight
    Of Yankees running rapidly.

Still on McDowell's farthest left,
The roar of cannon strikes one deaf,
Where furious Abe and Fiery Jeff
    Contend for death or victory.

The panic thickens—off, ye brave!
Throw down your arms! your bacon save!
And fly, with all your chivalry![4]

They even sang of First Manassas to the tune of Stephen Foster's "Oh, Susanna."

I come from old Manassas, with a pocket full of fun,
I killed forty Yankees with a single-barrelled gun;
It don't make niff-a-stifference to either you or I
Big Yankee, little Yankee, all run or die.

Because of the ill-fated attack on Big Bethel in 1861, there was ridicule of Butler, the "trickery, dickery, slickery Ben." One satiric poem was sung to the tune of "Yankee Doodle."

SONG: "GENERAL BUTLER"
Butler and I went out from camp,
    At Bethel to make Battle,
And then the Southrons whipt us back,
    Just like a drove of cattle.
        Come throw your swords and muskets down,
            You do not find them handy,
        Although the Yankees cannot fight,
            At running they're the dandy.

And then we got a monster gun,
    Which gives us satisfaction,
For seven miles are just the space
    That Yankees like in action.
        Come throw your swords, etc.

Whenever we go out to fight
    The Southron give us lickings,
But then we strive fo get revenge
    By stealing all their chickens.
        Come throw your swords, etc.

4 "Bull Run—A Parody," from "War Poetry of the South."

Old Butler stays in Fort Monroe,
    And listens to the firing,
And when his men have met defeat,
    He then goes out enquiring.
        Come throw your swords, etc.

To say that Butler will not fight,
    Is certainly no scandal,
For not a trophy he has gained,
    Except an old-pump-handle.
        Come throw your swords, etc.

During the Civil War in Richmond, Virginia, a group of poets, authors, musicians and artists organized themselves into what they called the Mosaic Club. This club had no officers, rules or objectives, but was "simply the clashing of bright minds in hospitable and cultured homes under stimulus of rare good cheer and rarer coffee." Meetings were held at the homes of society leaders of Richmond and the evening's program was liable to include music or charades or even creative writing. Writing poetry was an extremely popular pastime and the members particularly enjoyed lampooning Northern generals and leaders in rhyme. Many of the members were particularly gifted along these lines.

Brigadier General Pierre Gustave Toutant Beauregard was given command of the Confederate forces bombing Major Anderson's garrison at Fort Sumter. On June 29, 1861, he became commander of the Confederate Army of the Potomac. In 1862 he assumed command of the Army of the Mississippi. After the death of General Johnston at Shiloh, he remained at the head of the army until after the withdrawal from Corinth at the end of May. In 1863 he defended Charleston and, in 1864, with Lee, joined in the defense of Petersburg and Richmond. He commanded the Confederate forces in the Carolinas in 1865 and finally surrendered his army to General Sherman.

Major Williams B. Myers of the Confederate Army was said to have had a wit that was full of quaint satire. He had been given an ode which had been composed about the Confederate General Beauregard.

Oh! the North was evil-starred when she met thee, Beauregard,
For you fought her very hard with cannon and petard, Beauregard.
Beau canon, Beauregard! Beau soldat, Beauregard!
Beau sabreur! Beau frappeur! Beauregard! Beauregard!

With the true spirit of the Mosaic Club, he promptly submitted the following:

Yes! the North was scarred and barred, and she took it very hard,
When we trumped her winning card, Beauregard!
Beau Blagueur, Beauregard! Beau blesseur, Beauregard!
Beau Brummell, Beau Nash, Beau Hickman, Beauregard!

Major General Braxton Bragg, West Point graduate, was better known in military annals before 1861 than perhaps any of the other Southern leaders because of his brilliant record in the Mexican War. In the Civil War he distinguished himself first at Shiloh

111

and then by meritorious services afterward. But he proved no match for Rosecrans, Grant, or Sherman because of his delays. Flanked out of two strong positions, he missed the opportunity presented by Rosecrans' unduly separated forces and failed to crush the Federal Army of the Cumberland in detail as it advanced to the Battle of Chickamauga. The ultimate loss of Tennessee by the Confederates is attributed to this error.

The following is a stanza from Innes Randolph's poem detailing Bragg's defeat:

> And Bragg did well, for who can tell—
> What merely human mind could augur—
> That they would run from Lookout Mount,
> Who fought so well at Chickamauga?

Benjamin Franklin Butler was commander of the Department and Army of the Gulf in 1862 and of the Army of the James in 1864. With his army, he operated against Richmond in May and June. After the conquest of New Orleans, Ben Butler went out as commander of the army of occupation and became Civil Administrator of the town. He was despised by the Creoles, who are said to have made up a story that Butler would steal the silver spoons when he was invited out to dinner.

His "woman order" caused even the French and British to shudder and finally had to be rescinded. In it he ordered that "when any female shall . . . insult or show contempt for any officer or soldier of the United States, she shall be regarded and held liable to be treated as a woman of the town plying her avocation."

> Hey! Diddle Sutler, the dastard Ben Butler,
> Fought women, morn, evening and noon;
> And old Satan laughed, as hot brimstone he quaffed
> When the Beast ran away with the spoon!

And another flattering reference to Butler:
> Trickery, dickery, slickery Ben—
> Eluding and dodging the frighting men—
> Was never afraid of a matron or maid,
> But cent for no cotton or silver he paid!

A poem was written on Butler's departure from New Orleans, "The Ladies' Farewell to Brutal Butler," which began:

We fill this cup to one made up of beastliness alone.

General Joseph Hooker was one of the many able generals, such as McClellan, Porter, "Phil" Kearny, and others, who believed in fine equipment and glittering trappings. A handsome, well-dressed man, he used the costliest of housing accommodations and horse accoutrements and expected his staff officers to follow suit. Much money was spent at the outset of the war in giving the army as trim and smart an appearance as the finest European regiment. But there were no military roads in the United States and the pageantry of a European army was not adapted to the swamps and morasses, the mountain heights, and rocky roads over which the war was fought. By the end of the second year, the red

112

sash which set off his trimly buttoned coat was gone. The costly shoulder straps of gold embroidery had given place to metal substitutes and the "hundred-dollar housings" of the Grand Review in the fall of 1861 were left in the swamps or lost in battle.

> Joe Hooker had a nice tin sword;
> Jack bent it up one day.
> When Halleck heard at Washington,
> He wrote: "Come home and stay."

Dan Sickles shot Philip Barton Key for an "intrigue" with his wife.

> Yankee Sickles came to fight, and Dan was just a dandy;
> Quite quick to shoot when 'tother man had nary a pistol handy!
>
> Henceforth, when a fellow is kicked out of doors,
> He need never resent the disgrace,
> But exclaim: "My dear sir, I'm eternally yours,
> For assisting in changing my base!"

General George Brinton McClellan's failure to capture Richmond in the Peninsula Campaign in the spring of 1862, and his failure to pursue Lee after Antietam were the chief reasons for his being replaced in November, 1862, by General Ambrose Burnside. A Mosaic Club member jibed at his procrastination.

> Little McClellan sat eating a melon,
> The Chickahominy by.
> He stuck in a spade; and a long time delayed,
> Then cried: "What a great general am I!"

In June, 1862, General John Pope was called to Washington to assume command of the newly created Army of Virginia.

General Pope's immediate objectives were to make the capital secure, to advance toward Richmond and, if possible, to draw a portion of Lee's army away from McClellan.

When the Federal army put Bull Run between itself and Lee on the night of August 30, 1862, Pope's attempt to capture Richmond was turned into a Confederate advance upon Washington.

The next morning, orders came from General Halleck for the broken and demoralized army of Pope to fall back within the defenses of Washington. Large quantities of Federal stores were left to fall into the hands of Lee, and these were of great use in his advance into Maryland.

Throughout the North there was great consternation at Pope's defeat. When he reached Arlington Heights, he became aware of public indignation and begged to be relieved of his command. The President complied with his request and the disorganized remnants of the Army of the Potomac and the Army of Virginia were returned temporarily to McClellan.

The Rebels claimed that "Commissary Pope joined Commissary [General Nathaniel] Banks in the Confederate esteem and everything was branded U.S.A. except ourselves." Pope, of course, became one of the chief targets for lyrical brickbats.

> Little Be-Pope, he lost his hope
>   Jackson, the Rebel to find him:
> But he found him at last, and he ran very fast,
>   With his bully invaders behind him!
>
> John Pope came down to Dixie town, and thought
>   it very wise
> To sit down in a 'skeeter swamp and start at telling
>   lies.
> But when he found his lies were out, with all his
>   might and main,
> He changed his base to another place, and began—
>   to lie again.

After bloody Antietam, Stonewall Jackson's brigade drove the Yankees out of Winchester, Virginia. The boys young Mary Taylor knew so well came running by with the Yankees in full retreat before them. The Taylors were "all huddled up behind the big stone chimney to get out of the way of the bullets which were singing around the house all the time." As Rebel troops came by, Mary ran out, heedless of the danger, and, though their faces were black with powder from biting off the heads of cartridges, "there was many a Johnny Reb that got a kiss and it need not be said from whom."

But the Rebels did not stay long, for "back came the Yanks" and soon the town was again under the Union flag. The Federals were in high spirits for they had driven back the enemy, and that night at Mary's house they were making merry. She was called in to sing Rebel songs, which she was not at all loath to do at any time. Things went along pretty well as long as she confined her repertoire to numbers like "Maryland, My Maryland," and "The Bonny Blue Flag," but she struck up the taunt: (to the tune of "Old Dan Tucker"):

> Yi, Yi, you old Bull Runner
> Yi, Yi, you old Bull Runner
> Yi, Yi, you old Bull Runner
> Run ten miles to the tune of our gunners.
>
> Old Winfield Scott Bull Run did ford
> He rolled up his sleeves and he pulled out his sword
> He was so fat and his cheeks so puffin'
> That the first thing he knew, he didn't know nuthin'.
>
> Yi, Yi, you old Bull Runner . . .

After General Nathaniel P. Banks' defeat in 1862 in the First Battle of Winchester in the Shenandoah Valley, the Confederates couldn't resist poking fun at him.

> You know the Federal General Banks,
> Who came through Louisiana with his forty thousand Yanks;
> His object was to execute the abolition law,
> With as mongrel a horde of soldiers as creation ever saw;
> There were Irish and English, and Spanish and Dutch,

And Negroes and Yankees, and many more such,
All dressed out in blue coats and fine filigree—
But such a skedaddle you never did see!

Mother Lincoln's Melodies
(Parody of Mother Goose Rhymes)

Little Be-Pope
He lost his hope,
"Coz" Jackson, he couldn't find him.
He found him at last,
And ran very fast,
With his tail hanging down beside him.

Burnside, Burnside, whither doth thou wander
Upstream, downstream, like a crazy gander?

The man in the North
He pledged his troth,
To find a Richmond barber,
But the man in the South,
He mashed his mouth
At a place they called Cold Harbor.

Old Mother *Seward*
She went to the *Lee*-ward
To get her dog *Union* a bone.
She got to Manassas,
And saw them harass us
Lord! How Mother Seward did groan!

Pope and McDowell
Fighting for a town
Up jumped General Lee
And knocked 'em both down.

Yankee was a bad man, Yankee was a thief,
Yankee came to my house and stole a piece of beef;
I went to Yankee's house, Yankee, he had fled,
Caught him on the battlefield, and there I killed him dead.

From *Confederate Scrap-book, Southern Literary Messenger,* and *Illustrated News.*

IV
Envelopes and Stationery

Both the North and South began using envelope illustrations immediately after the Confederate attack on Fort Sumter. In the beginning they were graphic patriotic outbursts. The flag of the United States printed in colors was the first device. The Southerners followed with envelope flags showing seven stars and three broad stripes, with the middle white part reserved for the name and address. The national arms, mottoes, and patriotic phrases followed—"Liberty and Union," "The Flag of the Free," and "To Arms, Brave Southrons." Many envelopes printed at the outset appeared with the prophecy "I shall wave again over Sumter" under the flag of the Union. Individual states proclaimed their allegiances with emblems and slogans such as "For the Union" or "For Secession."

A vogue for portraits of men like Lincoln, Davis, Scott, Beauregard, Fremont, and Dix followed the loyalty-to-country craze. General Butler's moustache waved on thousands of letters with his patriotic statement, "Whatever our politics, the government must be sustained." A little later his term, "Contraband of War," applied to fugitive Negroes, was endlessly repeated. A popular cartoon depicted a master and his escaping slave. "Come back, you old black rascal," the master cries. "Can't come back now," the Negroes say, "dis chile contraban'."

Decorated envelopes became a means of propaganda resorted to by both North and South. "Death to traitors," cried the angry North to the rebels, while the South proudly filled their mails with pictures of "The Rebel Martha Washington" and "The Rebel George Washington." Later the words "The Southern Gentleman and Slaveholder" were added.

116

Before long the light touch in envelope illustrations vanished. As in the case of political cartoons, many of which were reproduced on envelopes, the tone grew bitter, the hatred more pronounced. Southern envelopes featured vicious jingles under the mastheads of Northern states, as in the case of Rhode Island.

> Thou little tiny Yankee creature,
> Contemptible in every feature,
> Crawl in thy hole and hide thy head;
> For Southrons brave count thee as dead.

Northern artists sketched a picture of a bottle of "Union Bitters" and "Doctor Scott's pills" under which appeared the following stanza:

> To cure *secession* and its ills,
> Take Dr. Scott's *cast iron pills;*
> Well mixed with *powder of saltpetre,*
> Apply it to each *"fire eater."*
> With *Union bitters* mix it clever,
> And *treason is* warned off forever.

Satire and caricature had a field day in the North and South. Beauregard became "Blowregard" to the North, and Butler "Bombastes" to the South. Jeff Davis, of course, was the popular Confederate target of Northern wits. He was hung in almost a dozen different ways with the artist's pencil. A black flag and death's head with the words, "Jeff Davis—His Mark," appeared in many variations. Davis' remark, "All we want is to be let alone," likewise served to inspire satirical expression such as the one featuring a tombstone with the wording, "Jeff Davis Alone." Another version interpreted the word "alone" as meaning a loan from Britain. There were many cartoons taunting Jeff Davis for not taking Washington. One, probably the most popular anti-Davis cartoon, was executed by Frank Beard and was reproduced on envelopes and used as a letterhead. This lithograph cartoon lampoons Davis' threat to take Washington. A bulldog with epaulettes and a military hat and side whiskers stands guard over a cut of prize beef labeled "Washington." A greyhound with the Confederate flag about his waist, a planter's hat on his head, and the name "Jeff" on his collar slinks off with tail between his legs. Behind him are a palmetto tree and a bale of cotton. Behind old General U.S. (in some versions, General Scott) are money bags, barrels of beef, corn, and flour, and the ominous mouth of a cannon. "Jeff, why don't you take it?" General U.S. asks.

The end of war was forecast by numerous designs such as Negroes piping and dancing "the playing out of secession," General Scott clutching a bunch of Confederate soldiers in an enormous fist, and one of a rope so twisted as to look like a skull is called "End of Secession."

Envelope illustrations, like all Civil War graphic humor, cast a sidelight on the progress of the war and the changing sentiments of the people. Good taste prevents the reprinting in this volume of many which embody and recreate the virulent prejudice and the deep-rooted bias of a hundred years ago in a way that no newspaperman would have dared to express in writing. The Rebellion Era comes to life with terrifying clarity and we can understand even if we cannot sympathize with much of the fanaticism and emotional upheaval that has persisted for over a century.

"You'll catch it when mother wakes up!"
S. C. Upham, 310 Chestnut St.

THREE CHEERS FOR
THE RED, WHITE AND BLUE.

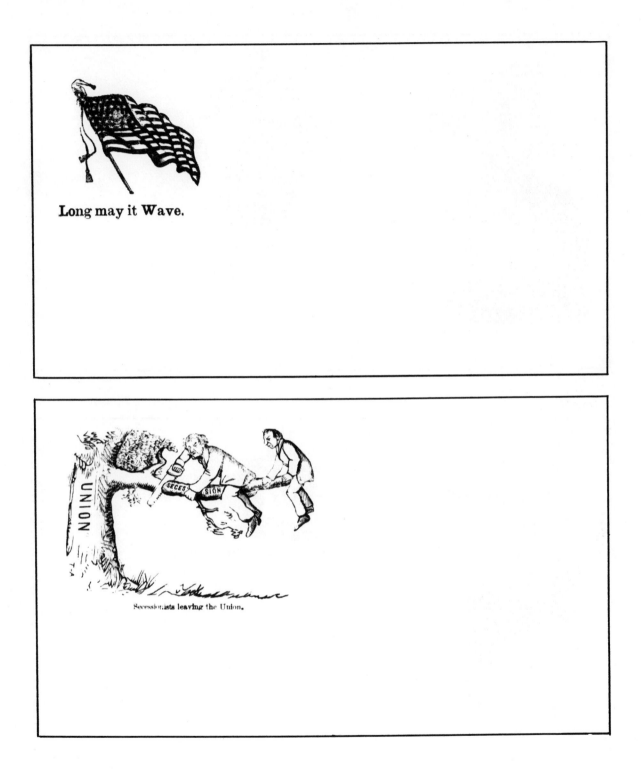

Long may it Wave.

Secessionists leaving the Union.

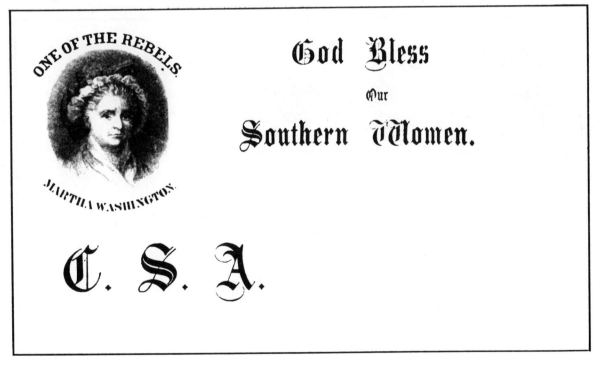

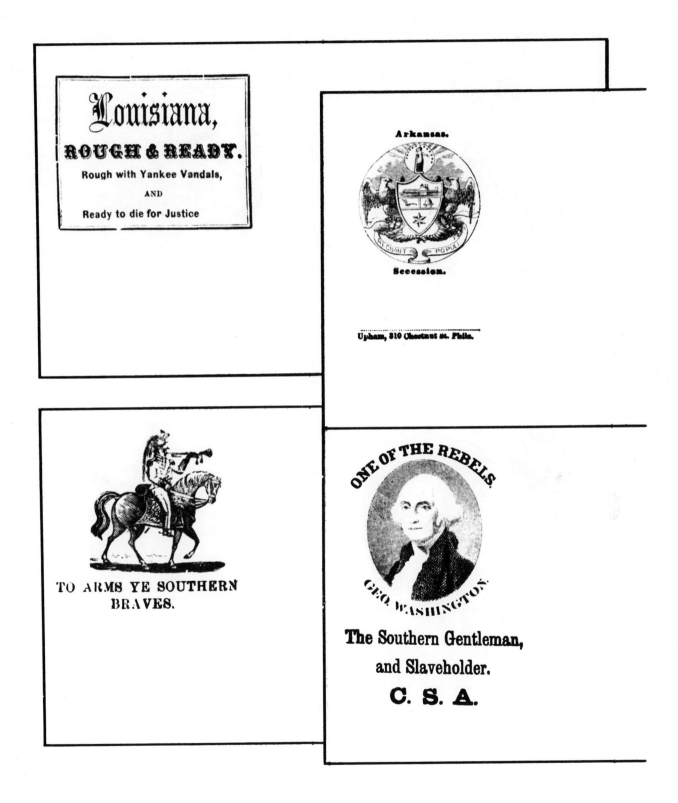

Louisiana,
ROUGH & READY.
Rough with Yankee Vandals,
AND
Ready to die for Justice

Arkansas.

Secession.

Upham, 310 Chestnut st. Phila.

TO ARMS YE SOUTHERN
BRAVES.

ONE OF THE REBELS.

GEO. WASHINGTON.

The Southern Gentleman,
and Slaveholder.
C. S. A.

Winfield Scott.

THE GREAT GEN. BUTLER,
KILLING VARMINTS.

Dictator Jeff finding he cannot have the
whole of Virginia, concludes to take only
a part.

No folly 'neath the sun surpasses
The folly of these suicidal Asses!

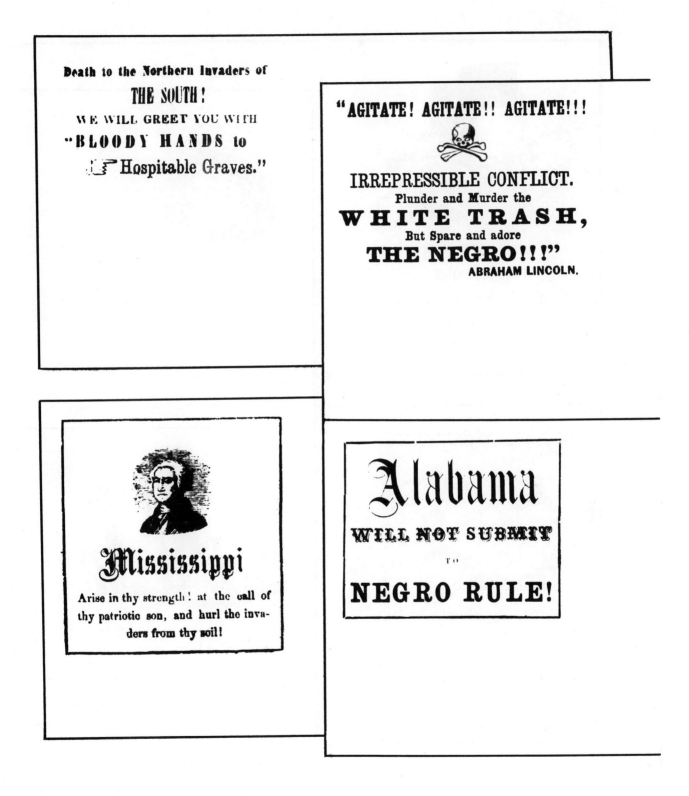

Death to the Northern Invaders of
THE SOUTH!
WE WILL GREET YOU WITH
"BLOODY HANDS to
☞Hospitable Graves."

"AGITATE! AGITATE!! AGITATE!!!

IRREPRESSIBLE CONFLICT.
Plunder and Murder the
WHITE TRASH,
But Spare and adore
THE NEGRO!!!"
ABRAHAM LINCOLN.

Mississippi
Arise in thy strength! at the call of
thy patriotic son, and hurl the invaders from thy soil!

Alabama
WILL NOT SUBMIT
TO
NEGRO RULE!

A SUGAR PLUMB
FOR LINCOLN
and his fellows in Iniquity.

Oregon.

For the Union.

Upham, 310 Chestnut St. Phila.

"Jewels" found at Alexandria, by the Federal Army; consisting of *Chains*, *Bracelets* and *Anklets*.

Supposed to have belonged to the "First Families" of Virginia.

S. C. Upham, 310 Chestnut St.

Old Blowregard will soon expire,
While thus he drills his shy MAN-*asscs*,
For they can never stand our fire,
While they feed on *Secession* grasses.

126

SECESSION PHYSIC CURE.

To cure *Secession* and its ills,
Take Dr. Scott's *Cast Iron Pills*;
Well mixed with *Powder* of *Saltpetre*,
Apply it to each "*Fire Eater.*"
With *Union Bitters*, mix it clever,
And *treason* is warned off forever.

JEFF. AND HIS PET.

☞ "**Through to Washington!**"

JEFF. DAVIS, APRIL 20, 1861.
[JULY 1, 1861.—NOT YET ARRIVED.]

WHY DON'T YOU TAKE IT?

127

A Fireman Zouave putting
out secession.

4

The original suggestion and adoption of the
Confederate Flag.

FLOYD OFF FOR THE SOUTH.

All that the Seceeding States ask is to be "let alone."

Latest News from the South.
"The Union feeling is increasing."

UNION GLUE

(Davis.)   (Wigfall.)   (Toombs.)   (Stephens.)

Mrs. Sippi.—"Didn't I tell you, Jeff., not to let
that stuff get into the house?"
Jeff.—"Couldn't help it, Mother, those Yankee
pedlars would leave it."

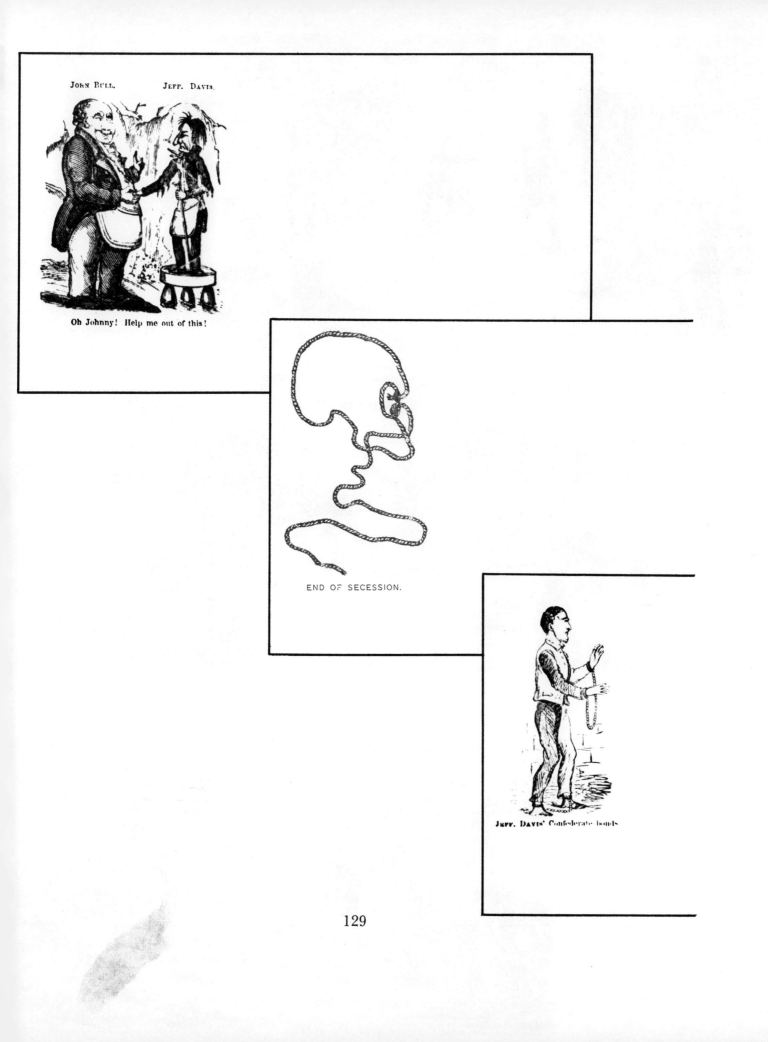

JOHN BULL.   JEFF. DAVIS.

Oh Johnny! Help me out of this!

END OF SECESSION.

JEFF. DAVIS' Confederate bonds

129

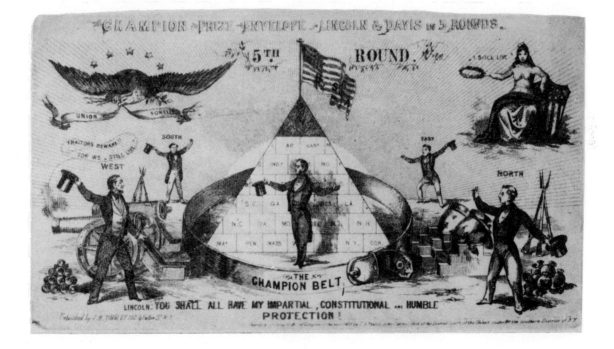

V
Literary Humor

Literary humor, like graphic humor, got off to a very slow start in colonial America. Our forebears were too preoccupied with eking out an existence and too bound by the strictures of Puritanism to find time for comedy.

By the eighteenth century some witty prose began to appear on the literary horizon in the South when William Byrd satirized the "motley population" of the North Carolina border. But it wasn't until the Revolutionary War that there began to be a vogue for satirical writings. This vogue reached its first great peak in the second quarter of the nineteenth century, when America finally developed a humor of her own. A spate of funnymen sprang up all over the country whose sole purpose in life was making Uncle Sam smile. In these somewhat low-brow, indigenous outpourings Americans quickly found a delightful means of escape, and laughter may be said to have reverberated throughout the land.

The rise in sales of comic books to extraordinary heights was not solely due to the enthusiasm of the American public, but resulted to a large extent from the popularity of the newspapers and their increasing influence. Before the days of syndicated news and humor, small-town newspapers copied news from other sheets. Editors of the more sophisticated press tolerated this practice if they were able to get in exchange some comic writing to enliven the pages of their own newspapers. "Fun in ink," says Quinn, "found the newspapers its chief medium of low-brow humor." A number of magazines like the *Spirit of the Times,* which contained many of the best humorous sketches of the South, sought to profit by these comic writings by reprinting them from the newspapers along with theatrical and other news.

The humor was for the most part regional and remained so until the outbreak of the Civil War, when there was a demand for a humor more national in scope. Back-country New England speech and manners were emphasized in a series of political articles as well as rural backwoods life in the South and West. These became the topics of many mirth-provoking sketches.

Among the first of the great literary comedians was Seba Smith of Maine whose *Letters of Major Jack Downing* were first published in 1830. Judge Thomas Chandler Haliburton began his series of short sketches from which emerged another famous Yankee character, Sam Slick the Clockmaker. Augustus Baldwin Longstreet, uncle of the Confederate General James Longstreet, came out with *Georgia Scenes,* a series of sketches on life in the Southeast. Johnson Jones Hooper, who in the fifties became a supporter of the avowed secessionist William Lowndes Yancey, and in 1861 Secretary and Librarian of the Confederate Congress, and private secretary to the Secretary of War, created the comic folk character of Captain Simon Suggs of North Carolina. George Horatio Derby, considered the "father" of the new school of American humor, wrote sketches signed "John Phoenix" which began to appear in 1850 and were later published in two volumes, *Phoenixiana* in 1855 and *Squibob Papers* in 1859. The *Partington Papers* and James Russell Lowell's *Bigelow Papers* in which Hosea Bigelow offered homely verses such as "Ez for war I call it murder there you hev it plain an' flat," remained popular through the Civil War period. George W. Bagby of Virginia became famous for *The Letters of Mozis Addums to Billy Ivvins* which were published in the *Southern Literary Messenger.* Mozis Addums was a provincial rustic from Southside Virginia who wrote of his adventures in the national capital.

The book considered the most significant antebellum volume of humor by a Southerner is *The Flush Times of Alabama and Missouri,* by Joseph Glover Baldwin, which contained a young lawyer's impressions of the booming Southwest with its "flush-time bars, boasters, liars, spreadeagle orators" and the like.

The outbreak of war provided writers as well as cartoonists with seemingly unlimited material. The war was present in all their writings. Many of the humorists took sides. George W. Bagby declared for a Southern Confederacy in December, 1860, and lost his Northern subscribers as well as many readers from the South. Discharged from the army after First Bull Run for physical disability, he returned to Richmond to edit the *Southern Literary Messenger,* which managed to survive despite rising prices and scarcity of ink in the South, and wrote critical articles about Jefferson Davis' administration.

Charles Graham Halpine, a versatile Irish journalist and poet who had been with General Hunter in South Carolina, introduced his war-inspired character, Private Mike O'Reilly, to readers of the *New York Herald,* and the sketches of this Irish private in the Union army became an immediate success. The series were subsequently published in two volumes as *Life and Adventures, Songs, Services and Speeches of Private Miles O'Reilly.* Robert Henry Newell's *Orpheus C. Kerr Papers* (the name is a pun on "office seeker") provided a sharp satire on civil and military affairs during the darker days of the war, and President Lincoln had many a laugh over this burlesque of the relentless office seeker of the time.

More and more humorists wrote in the guise of comic folk characters through whom they made sharp, shrewd observations about the critical period in which they were living, and took great delight in holding up to ridicule those individuals who reveled in self-importance.

David Ross Locke, a journeyman printer who turned to the writing of humor, was the creator of Petroleum Vesuvius Nasby; Charles Farrar Browne, another journeyman printer, created the character of Artemus Ward; and Charles H. Smith, a former mail carrier, Georgia lawyer, soldier, judge, and plantation owner, signed the name Bill Arp to his books.

Before the first Bill Arp letter was printed in the Rome, Georgia, *Confederacy* in April, 1861, Smith read it aloud to some friends whom he met on the street in Rome. Among the listeners was an illiterate ferryman, a small man known to be the champion fighter of the district and an intermittent drinker, and whose name happened to be William Arp. When Smith had finished his reading, Arp asked him what name he would use to sign the letters. Smith said he hadn't given it any thought; whereupon Arp said, "I wish you would put mine, for them's my sentiments."

In the beginning Bill Arp was represented as a Yankee sympathizer, but gradually he became an avowed Confederate who was ready to bet his last dollar on Dixie.

The Petroleum V. Nasby letters appeared in 1861 and were supposed to come from a backwoods preacher, postmaster, reformer, and chronic office seeker with Copperhead sympathies. Shortly afterward, Nasby settled in "Confedrit X Roads," Kentucky, where he drank whiskey and preached to Negro-hating Democrats. Locke, through his character of Petroleum Nasby, is said to have rendered great aid to the North. The preacher-postmaster proudly flaunted his unswerving loyalty to the simple principles of personal and political selfishness. His idea of luxury was a government job, a glass of whiskey, a clean shirt, and a dollar bill. This "rib-tickling irony" cheered the Northerners and confounded both Rebels and Southern sympathizers. Lincoln, who felt that Nast's drawings had helped recruit new soldiers, escaped from his heavy burdens in the Nasby letters. Grant stated that he "couldn't get through a Sunday without one." Secretary Boutwell is said to have attributed the Union victory to the combined efforts of the armed forces, the Republican Party, and the letters of Petroleum V. Nasby. According to Charles Sumner, Lincoln said of the Nasby letters: "For the genius to write these things I would gladly give up my office."

Communications from Charles Farrar Browne's brainchild, Artemus Ward, the first of the literary misspellers, first appeared in the *Cleveland Plain Dealer*. The character of Ward, the traveling showman who wrote letters to the press and displayed wax figures and a zoo here and there across the country, caught the public fancy at once both here and abroad. Browne became the only humorist known across the Atlantic. The British called Ward an intellectual Hans—the simpleton of the old German stories.

Ward had been strongly pro-slavery and anti-abolitionist in the beginning, but two months after the outbreak of war, he spoke against the South. *Artemus Ward His Book* (1862) is a pro-Union book with a caricature of Ward on the frontispiece delivering his "great Union speech." In the chapter "Artemus Ward in the Southern Confederacy," the showman tells of an altercation with a group of "Seseshers" when on a trip to Southern territory, which resulted in the confiscation of his show, and his subsequent arrest and imprisonment.

In creating Artemus Ward, Browne introduced an element of humor into American literature that was raised by Mark Twain to a higher level. It was a humor of the people which Lincoln understood so well and enjoyed wholeheartedly.

Lincoln's admiration for Ward met with the disgust of his Cabinet, particularly Secretary Stanton, as was evidenced at the famous Cabinet meeting of September 22, 1862.

At this meeting, which had been called for the purpose of considering the final form of the Emancipation Proclamation, Lincoln proceeded to read aloud two chapters from the recently published *Artemus Ward His Book* before starting the serious discussion. When he concluded the first, he laughed heartily but none of the others present joined in. Stanton was trying to make up his mind whether or not to "rise and leave the meeting abruptly" when, he later wrote Judge Hamilton Ward of New York, "Lincoln threw the book down, heaved a sigh and said: 'Gentlemen, why don't you laugh? With the fearful strain that is upon me night and day, if I did not laugh I should die, and you need this medicine as much as I do.' "

In seeking to provide their readers with a continuous supply of laughter, the literary humorists frequently resorted to verbal techniques to gain their interest. Dialect humor, anticlimax, extreme understatement, exaggeration, and the making of contradictory, inconsistent statements became part of the written form of American folk humor. Artemus Ward's use of contradiction, is well illustrated in his saying, "I tell you, feller-citizens, it would have bin ten dollars in Jeff Davis's pocket if he'd never been born!" The anticlimax is pointed up in Bill Arp's observation, "I like an affectionate familiarity between parents and children, though I want it understood I'm the boss of the family, that is, when Mrs. Arp is away from home."

The Civil War brought about a change in attitude toward the literary humorists. In the 1850's authors had still been inclined to deprecate their comic writings. Many, like Augustus Baldwin Longstreet of *Georgia Scenes* fame, were even ashamed of their work. Lincoln's predilection for the writings of the "lowly American humorists" did much to improve their status. In their articles and books, war-weary Americans found temporary relief from the daily anxieties, and sales of comic writings increased greatly. The shrewd observations and criticisms by men like Ward, Nasby, and Kerr on the political and military situations and their day-by-day commentary on the progress of the war were awaited with as much eagerness as was news from the battlefront. In a sense, says Blair, "they were news."

Humor became one of the orders of the day. Weeklies, dailies, and magazines all had their columns of anecdotes, humorous communiques, dramatic monologues, and comic sayings. Humorists reached new audiences and helped in the circulation of jokes by making public appearances. Many assumed the guise of their own literary characters. The pen name became the stage name, and the character became so identified with his creator that people used their names interchangeably. Charles Farrar Browne advertised his appearances with such advance notices as "Artemus Ward Will Speak a Piece." Ward, the showman of the written page, became the live displayer of waxworks on the lecture platform, and the identity of the author became secondary in importance.

As a result of this merging of identity, the criticism has been made that in time the literary creations were frequently out of character. In Browne's first book, for example, Ward is depicted by the illustrator, Henry L. Stephens, as the stout, bald, round-nosed, middle-aged owner and manager of a traveling circus. Browne himself was actually a lean person. But in *Artemus Ward His Travels* there is a picture of Ward strolling around the farm in which he resembles an early caricature of Browne himself, wherein the author was shown as a skinny man with high-bridged nose and drooping moustache.[1]

But such criticisms of their heroes of humor did not interfere with nor interrupt American laughter North or South during the four years of war. What people laughed at in the eighteen sixties and the situations they found so excruciatingly funny may not tickle the risibilities of present-day readers. For even though, as one historian puts it, "many a good thrust is left," time has taken the edge off much of the old humor. It is unlikely that any one of the onetime favorites could enjoy a complete resurgence of popularity. But as long as Americans believe in Uncle Sam and Yankee Doodle, there will be a place in our literary heritage for the folk humor of a century ago. To quote from Artemus Ward's Fourth of July oration: "In the langwidge of Mister Catterline to the Rummuns, I go, but perhaps I shall cum back agin."

From The Nasby Papers, by David Ross Locke.

HAS AN INTERVIEW WITH THE PRESIDENT

Church uv St. ——, Nov. 1, '63

I felt it my dooty to visit Washington. The misarable condishon the Dimocrisy find themselves into sinse the elecshen, makes it nassary that suthin be did, and therefore I determined to see wat cood be effectid by a persnel interview with the Presdent.

Interdoosin myself, I opened upon him delikitly, thus:

"Linkin," sez I, "ez a Dimocrat, a free-born Dimocrat, who is prepard to die with neetnis and dispatch, and on short notis, fer the inalienable rite uv free speech—knoin also that you er a goriller, a feendish ape, a thirster after blud, I speak."

"Speek on," sez he.

"I am a Ohio Dimocrat," sez I, "who hez repoodiatid Valandigum."

"Before or sinse the elecshin, did yoo repoodiate him?" sez he.

"Sinse," retortid I.

"I thot so," sed he. "I would hev dun it too, hed I bin you," continnered he with a goriller-like grin.

"We air now in favor uv a wiggerus prosecushen uv the war, and we want you to so alter yoor polisy that we kin act with yoo, corjelly," sez I.

"Say on," sez he.

"I will. We don't want yoo to change yoor polisy, materially. We air modrit. Anxshus to support yoo we ask yoo to adopt the follerin triflng changis:

Restoar to us our habis corpusses, as good ez new.

Arrest no moar men, wimmin and children, for opinyun's saik.

Repele the ojus confisticashen bill, wich irrytaits the Suthern mind and fires the Suthern hart.

Do away with drafts and conskripshens.

Revoak the Emansipashen proclamashen, and give bonds that you'll never ishoo a nother.

1 *Vanity Fair,* May 24, 1862.

Do away with tresury noats and sich, and pay nuthin but gold.

Protect our dawters frum nigger eqwality.

Disarm your nigger soljers, and send back the niggers to their owners to conciliate them.

Offer to assoom the war indetednis uv the South, and plej the Guverment to remoonerate our Suthrin brethren for the looses they hev sustaned in this onnatral war.

Call a convenshen uv Suthern men and sech gileless Northern men ez F. Peerce, J. Bookannun, Fernandough Wood and myself, to agree upon the terms uv re-union.

"Is that all," sez the goriller.

"No," sez I promptly. "Ez a garantee uv good faith to us, we shel insist that the best haff uv the orifises be given to Dimocrats who repoodiate Valandigum. Do this, Linkin, and yoo throw lard ile on the trubbled waters. Do this and yoo rally to yoor support thowsends uv noble Dimocrats, who went out uv offis with Bookannon, and hev bin gittin ther whisky on tick ever sinse. We hev maid sakrifises. We hev repoodiatid Valandigum— we care not ef he rots in Canaday—we are willin to jine the war party reservin to ourselves the poor privilidg uv dictatin how and on wat prinsipples it shel be carried on. Linkin! Goriller! Apr! I hev dun."

The President replide that he wood give the matter serious considerashen. He wood menshen the idee uv resinin to Seward, Chais and Blair, and wood addres a serculer to the Postmasters et settry, and see how menny uv em wood be willin to resine to accommodate Dimocrats. He hed no dout sevral wood do it to-wunst. "Is ther any littel thing I kin do fer you?"

Nothin pertikler. I wood accept a small Post orifis if sitooatid within ezy range uv a distilry. My politikle daze is well nigh over. Let me but see the old party wunst moar in the assendency—let these old eyes onct moar behold the Constooshn ez it is, the Union ez it wuz, and the Nigger ware he ought 2 be, and I will rap the mantel uv privit life arownd me, and go in2 delirum tremens happy. I hev no ambishen. I am in the sear and yaller leef. These whitnin lox, them sunken cheak, warn me that age and whisky hev dun ther perfeck work, and that I shell soon go hents. Linkin, scorn not my wurds. I have sed. Adoo."

So sayin I wavd my hand impressively and walked away.

Petroleum V. Nasby,
Paster uv sed Church, in charge.

From Artemus Ward His Book, by Charles Farrar Browne.

INTERVIEW WITH PRESIDENT LINCOLN

I hav no politics. Nary a one. I'm not in the bisiness. If I was I spose I should holler versiffrusly in the streets at nite and go home to Betsy Jane smellen of coal ile and gin, in the mornin. I should go to the Poles arly. I should stay there all day. I should see to it that my nabers was thar. I should git carriges to take the kripples, the infirm and the indignant thar. I should be on guard agin frauds and sich. I should be on the lookout for the infamus lise of the enemy, got up just *be4* elecshun for perlitical effeck. When all was over and my candydate was elected, I should move heving & arth—so to speak—until I got orfice, which if I didn't git a orfice I should turn round and abooze the Administration with all my mite and maine. But I'm not in the bisniss. I'm in a far more respectful bisniss nor what pollertics is. I wouldn't giv two cents to be a Congresser. The wuss insult I ever received was when sertin citizens of Baldinsville axed me to run fur the Legislater. Sez I, "My friends, dostest think I'd stoop to that there?" They turned as white as a sheet. I spoke in my most orfullest tones, & they knowd I wasn't to be trifled with. They slunked out of site to onct.

There4, havin no politics, I made bold to visit Old Abe at his humstid in Springfield. I found the old feller in his parler, surrounded by a perfeck swarm of orfice seekers. Knowin he had been capting of a flat boat on the roarin Mississippy I thought I'd address him in sailor lingo, so sez I "Old Abe, ahoy! Let out yer main-suls, reef hum the forecastle & throw yer jib-poop overboard! Shiver my timbers, my harty!" (N. B. This is ginuine mariner langwidge. I know, becawz I've seen sailor plays acted out by them New York theater fellers.) Old Abe lookt up quite cross & sez, "Send in yer petition by & by. I can't possibly look at it now. Indeed, I can't. It's onpossible, sir!"

"Mr. Linkin, who do you spect I air?" sed I.

"A orfice-seeker, to be sure?" sed he.

"Wall, sir," sed I, "yous never more mistaken in your life. You hain't gut a orfiss I'd take under no circumstances. I'm A. Ward. Wax figgers is my perfeshun. I'm the father of Twins, and they look like me—*both of them.* I cum to pay a friendly visit to the President eleck of the United States. If so be you wants to see me say so—if not, say so, & I'm orf like a jug handle."

"Mr. Ward, sit down. I am glad to see you, Sir."

"Repose in Abraham's Buzzum!" sed one of the orfice seekers, his idee bein to git orf a goak at my expense.

"Wall," sez I, "ef all you fellers repose in that there Buzzum thare'll be mity poor nussin for sum of you!" Whereupon Old Abe buttoned his weskit clear up and blusht like a maidin of sweet *16.* Jest at this pint of the conversation another swarm of orfice-seekers arrove & cum pilin into the parler. Sum wanted post orfices, sum wanted collectorships, sum wantid furrin missions, and all wanted sumthin. I thought Old Abe would go crazy. He hadn't more than had time to shake hands with 'em, before another tremenjis crowd cum porein onto his premises. His house and dooryard was now perfeckly overflowed with orfice seeksrs, all clameruss for a immejit interview with Old Abe. One man from Ohio, who had about seven inches of corn whisky into him, mistook me for Old Abe and addrest me as "The Pra-hayrie Flower of the west!" Thinks I, *you* want a offiss putty bad. Another man with a gold heded cane and a red nose told Old Abe he was "a seckind Washington & the pride of the Boundliss West."

Sez I, "Squire, you wouldn't take a small post-offis if you could git it, would you?"

Sez he, "A patrit is abuv them things, sir!"

"There's a putty big crop of patrits this season, ain't there Squire?" sez I, when *an-*

138

other crowd of offiss seekers pored in. The house, door-yard, barn & woodshed was now all full, and when *another* crowd cum I told 'em not to go away for want of room as the hog-pen was still empty. One patrit from a small town in Michygan went up on top the house, got into the chimney and slid down into the parler where Old Abe was endeverin to keep the hungry pack of orfice-seekers from chawin him up alive without benefit of clergy. The minit he reached the fire-place he jumpt up, brusht the soot out of his eyes, and yelled: "Don't make eny pintment at the Spunkville postoffiss till you've read my papers. All the respectful men in our town is signers to that there dockyment!"

"Good God!" cride Old Abe, "they cum upon me from the skize—down the chimneys, and from the bowels of the yearth!" He hadn't more'n got them words out of his delikit mouth before two fat offiss-seekers from Wisconsin, in endeverin to crawl atween his legs for the purpuss of applyin for the tollgateship at Milwawky, upsot the President eleck & he would hev gone sprawlin into the fire-place if I hadn't caught him in these arms. But I hadn't morn'n stood him up strate before another man cum crashin down the chimney, his head strikin me vilently agin the inards and prostratin my voluptoous form onto the floor. "Mr. Linkin," shoutid the ingatooated being, "my papers is signed by every clergy-man in our town, and likewise the skoolmaster!"

Sez I, "You egrjis ass," gittin up & brushin the dust from my eyes, "I'll sign your papers with this bunch of bones, if you don't be a little more keerful how you make my bread basket a depot in the futer. How do you like that air perfumery?" sez I, shuving my fist under his nose. "Them's the kind of papers *you* want!"

"But I workt hard for the ticket; I toiled night and day! The patrit should be rewarded!"

"Virtoo," sed I, holdin' the infatooated man by the coat-collar, "virtoo, sir, is its own reward. Look at me!" He did look at me, and qualed *be4* my gase. "The fact is," I continued, lookin' round on the hungry crowd, "there is scacely a offiss for every ile lamp carrid round durin' this campane. I wish thare was. I wish thare was furrin missions to be filled on varis lonely Islands where eppydemics rage incessantly, and if I was in Old Abe's place I'd send every mother's son of you to them. What air you here for?" I continnered, warmin up considerable, "can't you giv Abe a minit's peace? Don't you see he's worrid most to death! Go home, you miserable men, go home & till the sile! Go to peddlin tinware—go to choppin wood—go to bilin sope—stuff sessengers—black boots—git a clerkship on sum respectable manure cart—go round as original Swiss Bell Ringers—becum 'origenal and only' Campbell Minstrels—go to lecturin at 50 dollars a nite—imbark in the peanut bizness—*write for the Ledger*—saw off your legs and go round givin concerts, with techin appeals to a charitable public, printed on your handbills—anything for a honest living, but don't come round here drivin Old Abe crazy by your outrajis cuttings up! Go home. Stand not upon the order of your goin', but go to onct! If in five minits from this time," sez I pullin' out my new sixteen dollar huntin cased watch, and brandishin' it before their eyes, "Ef in five minits from this time a single sole of you remains on these here premises, I'll go out to my cage near by, and let my Boy Constructor loose! & ef he gits amung you, you'll think old Solferino has cum again and no mistake!" You ought to hev seen them scamper, Mr. Fair. They run orf as tho Satun his self was arter them with a red hot ten pronged pitch-fork. In five minits the premises was clear.

139

"How kin I ever repay you, Mr. Ward, for your kindness?" sed Old Abe, advancin and shakin me warmly by the hand. "How kin I ever repay you, sir?"

"By givin the whole country a good, sound administration. By poerin' ile upon the troubled waturs, North and South. By pursooin' a patriotic, firm, and just course, and then if any State wants to secede, let 'em Secesh!"

"How bout my Cabinit, Mister Ward?" sed Abe.

"Fill it up with Showmen sir! Showmen is devoid of politics. They hain't got any principles! They know how to cater for the public. They know what the public wants, North & South. Showmen, sir, is honest men. If you doubt their literary ability, look at their posters, and see small bills! Ef you want a Cabinit as is a Cabinit fill it up with showmen, but don't call on me. The moral wax figger perfeshun mustn't be permitted to go down while there's a drop of blood in these vains! A. Linkin, I wish you well! Ef Powers or Walcutt was to pick out a model for a beautiful man, I scarcely think they'd sculp you; but ef you do the fair thing by your country you'll make as putty a angel as any of us! A. Linkin, use the talents which Nature has put into you judishusly and firmly, and all will be well! A. Linkin, adoo!"

He shook me cordyully by the hand—we exchanged picters, so we could gaze upon each others liniments when far away from one another—he at the hellum of the ship of State, and I at the hellum of the show bizniss—admittance only 15 cents.

Excerpts from The Orpheus C. Kerr Papers, Third Series, by Robert Henry Newell.

CHAPTER IV

Describing the South in twelve lines, defining the citizen's first duty, and reciting a parody.

Washington, D.C., April ——, 1861.

The chivalrous South, my boy, has taken Fort Sumter, and only wants to be "let alone." Some things of a Southern sort I like, my boy; Southdown mutton is fit for the gods, and Southside particular is liquid sunshine for the heart; but the whole country was growing tired of new South wails before this, and my present comprehensive estimate of all there is of Dixie may be summed up in twelve straight lines, under the general heading of

REPUDIATION

'Neath a ragged palmetto a Southerner sat,
A-twisting the band of his Panama hat,
And trying to lighten his mind of a load
By humming the words of the following ode:
    "Oh! for a nigger, and oh! for a whip;
    Oh! for a cocktail, and oh! for a nip;
    Oh! for a shot at old Greeley and Beecher;
    Oh! for a crack at a Yankee school-teacher;
    Oh! for a captain, and oh! for a ship;
    Oh! for a cargo of niggers each trip."
And so he kept oh-ing for all he had not,
Not contented with owing for all that he'd got.

In view of the impending conflict, it is the duty of every American citizen, who has nothing else to do, to take up his abode in the capital of this agonized Republic, and give the Cabinet the sanction of his presence. Some base child of treason may intimate that Washington is not quite large enough to hold every American citizen; but I'm satisfied that, if all the Democrats could have one good washing, they would shrink so that you might put the whole blessed party into an ordinary custom house. Some of the Republicans are pretty large chaps for their size, but Jeff Davis thinks they can be "taken in" easily enough to make them contract like sponges out of water. The city is full of Western chaps, at present, who look as if they had not got beyond gruel diet yet. Every soul of them knew old Abe when he was a child, and one old boy can even remember going for a doctor when his mother was born. I met one of them the other day (he is after the Moose-hicmagunticook post-office), and his anecdotes of the President's boyhood brought tears to my eyes, and several tumblers to my lips. He says, that when Abe was an infant of sixteen, he split so many rails that his whole county looked like a wholesale lumber-yard for a week; and that when he took to flat-boating, he was so tall and straight, that a fellow once took him for a smoke-stack on a steamboat, and didn't find out his mistake until he tried to kindle a fire under him. Once, while Abe was practising as a lawyer, he defended a man for stealing a horse, and was so eloquent in proving that his client was an honest victim of false suspicion, that the deeply affected victim made him a present of the horse as soon as he was acquitted. I tell you what, my boy, if Abe pays a post-office for every story of his childhood that's told, the mail department of this glorious nation will be so large that a letter smaller than a two-story house would get lost in it.

From Bill Arp's Correspondence, by Charles Henry Smith (1826-1903).

Rome, Ga., Aprile 1861

BILL ARP TO ABE LINKHORN

Mr. Linkhorn—Sur: These are to inform you that we are all well, and hope these lines may find you in statue ko. We received your proklamation, and as you have put us on very short notis, a few of us boys have konkluded to write you, and ax for a little more time. The fact is, we are most obleeged to have a few more days, for the way things are happening, it is utterly onpossible for us to disperse in twenty days. Old Virginy, and Tennessee, and North Callina, are continually aggravatin us into tumults and carousements, and a body can't disperse until you put a stop to sich onruly condukt on their part. I tried my darndest yesterday to disperse and retire, but it was no go; and besides, your marshal here ain't doing a darned thing—he don't read the riot act, nor remonstrate, nor nothing, and ought to be turned out. If you konklude to do so, I am orthorized to rekummend to you Col. Gibbons or Mr. McLung, who would attend to the bizniss as well as most anybody.

The fact is, the boys round here want watchin, or they'll take sumthin. A few days ago I heard they surrounded two of our best citizens, because they was named Fort and Sumter. Most of em are so hot that they fairly siz when you pour water on em, and that's the way they make up their military companies here now—when a man applies to jine the volunteers, they sprinkle him, and if he sizzes they take him, and if he don't they don't.

Mr. Linkhorn, sur, privately speakin, I'm afeerd I'll git in a tite place here among these bloods, and have to slope out of it, and I would like to have your Skotch cap and kloak that you traveled in to Washington. I suppose you wouldn't be likely to use the same disgize agin, when you left, and therefore I would propose to swap. I am five feet five, and could git my plow breeches and coat to you in eight or ten days if you can wait that long. I want you to write to me immegitly about things generally, and let us know where-abouts you intend to do your fitin. Your proklamation says somethin about taking posses-sion of all the private property at "All Hazards." We can't find no such place on the map. I thot it must be about Charleston, or Savannah, or Harper's Ferry, but they say it ain't anywhere down South. One man said it was a little Faktory on an iland in Lake Champlain, where they make sand bags. My opinion is, that sand bag bizness won't pay, and it is a great waste of money. Our boys here carry there sand in there gizzards, where it keeps better, and is always handy. I'm afeered your Government is givin you and your kangaroo a great deal of onnecessary trubbul, and my humble advice is, if things don't work better soon, you'd better grease it, or trade the darned old thing off. I'd show you a slite-of-hand trick that would change the whole concern into buttons quick. If you don't trade or do sumthin else with it soon, it will spile or die on your hands, sertain.

Give my respekts to Bill Seward and the other members of the kangaroo. What's Han-nibal doin? I don't hear anything from him nowadays.

Yours, with care,
Bill Arp

P.S. If you can possibly extend that order to thirty days, do so. We have sent you a *check* at Harper's Ferry (who keeps that darnd old Ferry now? its giving us a heap of trubble), but if you positively won't extend, we'll send you a check drawn by Jeff Davis, Borygard endorser, payable on sight anywhere.

Yours,
B. A.[1]

From The Life and Adventures, Songs, Services and Speeches of Private Miles O'Reilly (47th Regiment, New York Volunteers). By Charles Graham Halpine with comic illustra-tions by Mullen.

Return of Private Miles O'Reilly.—His Reception in New York.

New York Herald, Oct., 1868.

Private Miles O'Reilly, Forty-seventh Regiment New York Volunteers, having been pardoned by the President for his breach of decorum in publishing songs relative to the joint naval and military operations against Charleston, came to this city in the "Arago" last week, having been given a thirty days' furlough by General Gillmore, at the end of which time he will proceed to Washington, and report to the President for special duty. Private O'Reilly was received by a large party of distinguished friends off Sandy Hook, on board the steam yacht of our excellent Port Surveyor, Mr. Rufus F. Andrews, who seems

[1]Courtesy of The New York Historical Society, New York City.

always ready to give both his vessel and his time to such festivities. Excellent speeches were made by General Daniel E. Sickles, Mr. James T. Brady, John Van Buren, Wm. E. Robinson, Commodore Joseph Hoxie, Judge Charles P. Daly, Daniel Devlin, and others; while Dr. Carmichael, Mr. John Savage, Mr. Stephen C. Massett, Mr. Barney Williams, and several celebrated songsters, amateur and professional, favored the company with patriotic and expressive melodies as the good vessel steamed up the Hudson on a brief pleasure trip.

Private O'Reilly is now staying at the residence of his cousin, Mr. James O'Reilly, quite a prominent Democratic politician in the Sixteenth Ward, who is at present employed in the City Inspector's department. The military minstrel's health seems to have suffered somewhat from the rigors of his late confinement on Morris Island; but his spirits remain as high as ever, and his letter of versified thanks to Mr. Lincoln is one of the most truly humorous things we have seen for many days. Of this production we can only give two verses—the first and second—O'Reilly saying that the balance (which treats liberally of the Cabinet difficulties and the "succession"), cannot appear until the President gives his consent to its publication—Private Miles declaring that he has had his full share of punishment for publishing rhymes without authority, and that he is resolved never knowingly to be caught in the same bad scrape again. His letter to the President begins:

Long life to you, Misther Lincoln!
 May you die both late an' aisy;
An' whin you lie wid the top of aich toe
 Turned up to the roots of a daisy,
May this be your epitaph, nately writ—
 "Though thraitors abused him vilely,
He was honest an' kindly, he loved a joke,
 An' he pardoned Miles O'Reilly!"
And for this same act while I've breath in me lungs
 Or a heart in me body beatin',
It's "long life to you, misther Lincoln!"
 That meself will keep repeatin':
If you ain't the handsomest man in the world
 You've done handsome by me, an' highly;
And your name to poshterity will go down
 Arm in arm wid Miles O'Reilly!

Excerpts from MacPherson, the great Confederate philosopher and Southern blower. By Alfred C. Hills.

THE LETTERS OF JAMES B. MACPHERSON.
CHAPTER I
Free Trade with the Rebels

Note: Madisonville is a town situated on the Tchefuncta river, near Lake Pontchartrain, and was within the rebel lines at the time these letters were written, as it is, in fact, at the present time. The people were known to be destitute of many of the necessaries of life, and the secessionists of New Orleans made a strong effort to induce the authorities to permit free trade across the lake, on the ground that humanity required it, and that the people were noncombatants. The *Daily Picayune* advocated this theory, and a writer, signing himself "Observer," published a communication in that paper urging its adoption by the authorities. The notion appeared too absurd to be treated seriously, and the author attempted to exhibit it in this light in the following letter, which appeared in *The Era,* February 17, 1863.

Madisonville, La.,
Sunday Evening, February 15.

Sir: I have a wife and twelve children, all of them sons except the wife. Nine of them are in the Confederate service, and so am I. The other three are not in the service, because one of them is only three years old, but he will probably be old enough to join the army before the United States are crushed. Another one has lost a leg in the war, so that he can't march; and the other one is idiotic. I am home on a furlough, and find my wife and three sons bad enough off. They are destitute of many of the necessaries of life, and for my part I don't know what they will do.

I think the United States ought to supply them with food. They are noncombatants, and there is no chance that any of them will ever fight except the youngest; and stipulation might be made that he should not eat any of the food sent over, if that should be deemed necessary.

So long as I and the nine able-bodied boys stay in the Confederate army, it will be necessary to have the rest of the family receive supplies from New Orleans; and humanity and philanthropy demand that trade should be allowed.

I was pleased to read in this morning's *Picayune,* a communication from Mr. Observer, on this point. He proposes to send salt and other indispensable articles, and says he would go into the business himself, if he had the means, and could get the necessary authority. I hope he will go into it at once, as we need the salt much, and the indispensable articles would also come in handy. He can make a good thing of it, as we are willing to pay a large price for salt, flour, quinine, clothing, cotton-cards, etc., all of which will bring a larger price here than Observer will have to give for them in New Orleans. I would pay a large price for what my family needs, as I could fight a great deal better if I knew the folks were comfortable at home. By all means let some one lend Mr. Observer the capital if he hasn't got it, for there is no reason why noncombatants shouldn't be fed.

Yours, sincerely,
James B. Macpherson

P.S. While you are about it, tell Observer to bring me an English rifle, with a cartridge box, and a hundred rounds of ammunition.

J. B. M.

Excerpts from Major Jack Downing

I.

The Major Announces that he "Still Lives"—The Reason why he has not Spoken before —Writes to "President Linkin," who at once Sends for him—How Lincoln Shakes Hands— His Troubles—The Major's Advice—Lincoln to get an "Appintment on Gineral McClellan's Staff"—A Story About Old Rye, from Mr. Lincoln.

Washington, Feb. 4th, 1862.

To the Editors of the Cawcashin, New York:

Surs: I spose eenamost everybody believed I wus ded, 'cause they aint seen any letters of mine in the papers for a good while. But it taint so. I'me alive, and though I can't kick quite as spry as I used to, yet I kin ride a hossback about as good as I could twenty year ago. I am now nigh on eighty years old, and yet, except getting tuckered out easier than I used to, I believe I feel jest about as smart as I did when I was a boy. The last letters I writ for the papers was about ten years ago, when I went all around the country with Kossoot, and showed him the sights. Sence then I've been livin' in Downingville, county of Penobscot, State of Maine, and enjoyin' in gineral a good state of helth. But if the public haint heard from me, it taint because I wasn't keepin' a close eye on matters and things. But the sartin truth is jest here: I seen, a good while ago, how things was shapin'. I told Kossoot that the pesky Abolishunests would ruin him, and they did, and I've knowed for a long time that thay would run this country off the Dimokratic track and smash it all to flinders. Wall, they've done it. You may wunder why I haint spoke and told the country all this before. Wall, the reason is jest here: I saw that the breechin' was broke some years ago, and there is no use of talkin or hollerin "Whoa! whoa!" after that. I've seen the laziest old hoss that ever lived kick and run like all possessed as soon as the shafts tetched his heels and that's jest the condishun we've been in in this country for some time. We've been kickin' and runnin' and raisin' the old scratch generally for ten years, all about these darned kinky-heded niggers. As there is no use of tryin' to stop a runaway hoss after the breechin' brakes until he gets to the bottom of the hill, so there is no use of talkin' to a country while it is goin in the same direcshun. Didn't Noah preech to a hull generashun of aunty-Deluvens, and it warn't any use. They larfed him rite in the face; and cum round him and axed what he intended to do with a boat full of chicken coops hoss stables, and so on. And at last, when the rain begun to cum down like all possessed, they swore it "warn't much of a freshet arter all." Wal, jest so it is with this generashun. I spect the aunty-slaveryites are shum relashun to the anty-Deluvens, and that accounts for their simelur behaveyur.

But I think that we've got most to the bottom of the hill now, and it is about time to get things rited up in some short of shape. Havin come to this conclushin, about ten days ago, I wrote a letter to President Linkin, tellin him how that Gineral Jackson's old friend was yet alive, and that if he wanted my sarvices or advice I would come on to Washington and help him thro'. Wal, I got a letter rite back, in which Linkin said he "was tickled all into a heap to hear that Gineral Jackson's old friend, Major Jack Downing, was still alive, and that he wanted him to cum on to Washington rite off." So I put off, like shot off a shovel, and dident even stop in New York a day, or I should have called to see you. The truth is, I'me darn glad I cum. I went rite up to the White House, which looks as nateral as when Gineral Jackson and I lived there, and sent in my keerd. In a minnit the sarvent cum back,

145

and ses he, "Walk up." I went up-stairs, and then into Linkin's room, and you never seed a feller gladder to see a man than he was to see me. He got hold of my hand, and ses he, "Major, you are a brick. I've thought a thousand times that if I only had such a friend as Gineral Jackson had in you, that I could git along as easy as snuff. But ye see, Major, all these pollyticens are a set of tarnel hyppercrits, and I hate 'em." And he kept talkin and shakin my hand until I thot hed sprain my rist. So I ses, "Mr. Linkin, I can't stand hard squeezin as well as I used to, so don't hold on quite so hard." Then he apologized, and said "how he was so anxus to see me that he was almost crazy." I told him that "I hed cum to see him through, jist as I did Gineral Jackson, and that I would stick by him as long as there was a shirt to his back, if he would only do rite."

"Wal," ses he, "Major, that is jist what I want to do. But it's awful hard work to tell what is rite. Here I am pulled first one way and then tother."

"Now," ses I, "Linkin, I'me goin to talk rite out to you. The fact is, there never was a President that had such a party at his back as you've got. You see it's made up of Old Whigs, Abolitionists and free sile Dimmycrats. Now, there ain't any more rale mixture to this conglommyrate than there is to ile and water. The truth is, I'd as soon take Illinoy muck, and Jersey mud, and Massachusetts cobble stuns to make a fine coat mortar of, as I would to get such materials to put into a pollytical party. You can't never make them gee."

"Wal," ses he, "Major, I've begun to think that way myself. The truth is, I've been trying all summer to please everybody, and the more I try to do it, the more I don't succeed. When I am conservative, then the aunty-slaveryites come down on me like all possessed, with old Horass Greelie at their hed. When I go a little t'other way, then the conservatives and my old neighbors, the Kentuckians, they come down upon me, and that takes me right off the handle. I can't stand it. So you see, Major, I'm in hot water all the time."

"I see your troubles," ses I, "Mr. Linkin, and I'll have to look about some days afore I can get the exact hang of things, but as soon as I do, I'll make matters as clear as a pipe-stem."

"Wal," ses he, "Major, I want you to make yourself at hum, and jist call for anything you want."

I told him there warn't but two things that I keered for except victuals, and that was a pipe and tobacco, and jist a little old rye, now and then. That gave him the hint, and Linkin rang a bell, and a sneakin' lookin feller, in putty bad clothes, made his appearance. Linkin told him to get some tobacco and the black bottle. The feller soon fetched them in, and Linkin said that that "old rye" was twenty years old, and jist about the best licker he ever drank. He said he found it very good to quiet his nerves after a hard day's work. I told him that that was jist what Gineral Jackson always said. "Did he?" ses Linkin; "wal," ses he, "I only want to imitate Jackson. That would be glory enough for me."

"Wal, now," ses I, "Linkin, the first thing you must do, in order to be poplar, is to be a military man. That was the way Jackson got up in the world, and if I had never been a Major, I really believe I'd never been heerd of out of Downingville. Now, jist as soon as the people believe you are an officer, with epaulettes on, they'll think you are the greatest man that ever lived."

"Wal," ses Linkin, "I think that is a fust chop idea. How can it be carried out?"

"Wal," ses I, "you must get an appintment on Gin. McClellan's staff! with the rank of Kernal. Nothing short of that will answer at all. Then get a splendid uniform and a fine hoss, and have the papers describe them, and get up pictures, and the shop-keepers will have their windows full of lithegraphs, and in six months you will be the most poplar man in the country, and sure to be next President."

When I sed that, he jumped right up, and ses he, "Major, you're worth your weight in gold. You have hit the nail right on the head. I'll do it; by the Eternal, I'll settle this trouble yet!"

"That's the talk," ses I, "Jist put your foot down, and let it stay down, and you may be sure it will all come out right."

Then Linkin said to me, ses he, "Major take a good swig of this old rye. If you feel sick, have got a cold or looseness in the bowells, or need physic, or have got the rheumatiz, or pane in the back, or the headache, there's nothin like old rye to set you on your pins just as good as new. Why, Major, let me tell you a story. There was a feller out West, who got a splinter in his foot. He was splittin' rails one day, and the axe glanced off, and sent a piece of Chesnut timber in his heel, about as big as an axe-handle. Wal, he tried everything on 'arth. Finally, he came to me, and I gave him some old rye, and the splinter came out in five minutes afterwards."

"Wal," ses I, "Linkin, that is a purty good story, and old rye is a capital drink, but as for medicin', give me my old stuff, elderberry bark tea. It's handy to use. Scrape it downwards, and it makes a fust-rate fisic, and scrape it upwards it is a capital emetic. The only danger is that when you scrape it round-about-ways, it stirs up a young earth-quake in a man's bowells equal to Mount Vesuvius on a bust. Kossoot made a mistake of this once, and I had to hed him up in a flour barrel, and roll him round the room afore he cum to."

When Linkin heard how I rolled Kossoot in a flour barrel, he laid back and larfed as hard as he could roar, and said, he hadn't felt in such good spirits since he had been in Washington.

I told him he mustn't get the blews, and that I should cheer him up. Then he tuk me by the han' and bid me a very feelin goodnight, and the feller in bad clothes showed me to my room. I slept as sound as a bug un a rug all night, and feel good as new this mornin.'

I shall soon get things straightened out here, I hope, and if anything interestin' happens, you may hear from me agin.

Your friend till death,
Major Jack Downing.

VI
Anecdotes and Other
Comic Briefs

President Lincoln was responsible for many jokes. On one occasion, Senator Wade came to him and said:

"I tell you, Mr. President, that unless a proposition for emancipation is adopted by the government, we will all go to the devil. At this very moment we are not over one mile from hell."

"Perhaps not," said Mr. Lincoln, "as I believe that is just about the distance from here to the Capitol, where you gentlemen are in session."

On another occasion, at a reception, when the crowd of citizens and soldiers was surging through the salons of the White House, evidently controlled by the somewhat brusque Western element, a gentleman said to him:

"Mr. President, you must diminish the number of your friends, or Congress must enlarge this edifice!"

"Well," promptly replied Mr. Lincoln, "I have no idea of diminishing the number of my friends; but the only question with me now is whether it will be best to have the building stretched or split."

At one of these receptions, when a paymaster in full major's uniform was introduced, he said:

"Being here, Mr. Lincoln, I thought I would call and pay my respects."

"From the complaints made by the soldiers," responded the President, "I guess that is all any of you do pay."

Ward Lamon, when Lincoln had appointed him Marshal of the District of Columbia, accidentally found himself in a street fight, and, in restoring peace, he struck one of the belligerents with his fist, a weapon with which he was notoriously familiar. The blow was a harder one than Lamon intended, for the fellow was knocked senseless, taken up unconscious, and lay for some hours on the border of life and death. Lamon was alarmed, and the next morning reported the affair to the President.

"I am astonished at you, Ward," said Mr. Lincoln, "you ought to have known better. Hereafter, when you have to hit a man, use a club and not your fist."

Stonewall Jackson found old Miles, a Virginia bridgebuilder, a handy person to have around. Bridges were swept away so often by floods or burned by the enemy that Miles was as necessary to the Confederate army as Jackson himself. One day the Union troops had retreated and burned a bridge across the Shenandoah. Jackson, determined to follow them, summoned Miles.

"You must put all your men on that bridge," he said. "They must work all night, and the bridge must be completed by daylight. My engineer will furnish you with the plan, and you can go right ahead."

Early next morning Jackson, in a very doubtful frame of mind, met the old bridgebuilder.

"Well," said the general, "did the engineer give you the plan for the bridge?"

"General," returned Miles slowly, "the bridge is done. I don't know whether the pictur' is or not."

From that time forth, General Jackson is said to have allowed Miles to build the bridges after his own fashion, without annoying him with "picturs."

Taking of Fort Sumter

We have reason to believe that the following were the actual telegrams which passed between General Beauregard, Major Anderson, and L. P. Walker, the Secessionist Secretary of War:

(No. 1.)
To L. P. Walker, Secretary of War.

"An authorized messenger from President Lincoln has just informed General Pickens and myself that several hampers of Canvas-back Ducks, Wild Turkeys, Corn Cakes, and materials for brandy-smashes and cock-tails will be sent to Fort Sumter, peaceably or otherwise.

Charleston, April 8.   G. F. Beauregard."

(No. 2.)
General G. F. Beauregard, Charleston

"Stop 'em! Keep what you like, and send the rest to me. Give Major Anderson notice to quit. If that won't do, put your men in possession.

Montgomery, April 10.   L. P. Walker, Secretary of War."

149

(No. 3.)

L. P. Walker, Secretary of War

"Luncheon is ordered at 12 o'clock.

Charleston, April 10.   G. F. Beauregard."

(No. 4.)

L. P. Walker, Secretary of War

"Demand sent at 12—Allowed till 6 o'clock for dinner.

Charleston, April 11.   G. F. Beauregard."

(No. 5.)

General Beauregard, Charleston.

"Telegraph what Major Anderson says to that.

Montgomery, April 11.   L. P. Walker, Secretary of War."

(No. 6.)

L. P. Walker, Secretary of War

"Major Anderson replies: 'I have the honour to acknowledge the receipt of your communication, demanding me to evacuate this fort, and to dine before six, without waiting to receive supplies. I regret that my obligations to my Government, and my own digestive organs, prevent my compliance.' He adds, 'I will await the first shot, and then drink your good-health in a brandy-smash.'

Charleston, April 11.   G. F. Beauregard."

(No. 7.)

General Beauregard, Charleston.

"Fire away (but don't hurt anybody), unless Major Anderson will send you the latch-key of the Fort.

L. P. Walker, Secretary of War."

(No. 8.)

L. P. Walker, Secretary of War

"He won't consent. He's not such a fool as you think.

Charleston, April 12.   G. F. Beauregard."

The bombardment then commenced, and after 40 hours' gallant resistance, Major Anderson having nothing but his umbrella left to cover him, hoisted a flag of truce.

(No. 9.)

Major Anderson, Gingham Umbrella,
Fort Sumter.

"I see your condition through my telescope. We have intercepted your supplies. Give in, like a good fellow, and bring your garrison to dinner, and beds afterwards. Nobody injured, I hope?

G. F. Beauregard."

150

General Beauregard, Charleston.

"Major Anderson presents his compliments to General G. F. Beauregard, and has much pleasure in accepting his kind invitation to dinner and beds. As no one is hurt, Major Anderson fears he shall put General B. F. Beauregard to some inconvenience, the party being a large one.   Anderson, Major."

And so ended the first (and we trust the last) engagement of the American Civil War. (*Punch,* Vol. XL.)

What the Southern Leaders Are Fighting For

General Garfield, late of the Army of Cumberland, spoke at the great Union meeting in Baltimore on Wednesday evening, Nov. 11, 1863, taking a strong anti-slavery ground. Among other things, he said:

"For these two and a half years I have been where I could see something of those men who are attempting to bear down our country. I have talked with many of them, and they are bold to avow that they propose to build up, as the Right Reverend General Polk told me, not a common Government, but a Government of gentlemen, of men of money, men of brains, who hold slaves; a Government such as the people of the Old World will not laugh at. They intend to have their Count Bragg and their My Lord Beauregard. You mud-sills, who rejoice that God has given you strong hands and stout hearts—who were not born with silver spoons in your mouths—are to be mud-sills a long time. This is the dream these fanatic men have before them."

How I Passed the Doctor—An Incident during the Draft

The other day Chief Engineer Dean, of the Fire Department, called at the office where I make shoes for a living, and handed me a big white envelope, notifying me that I was drafted and must report myself for examination, at Lawrence, on the 18th of August.

Now I consider it the duty of every citizen to give his life, if need be, for the defence of his country, so on the morning of the eventful 18th, I put on a clean shirt and my Sunday clothes, and started for Lawrence, to see if I could get exempted.

Lawrence is situated on the Merrimac river, and its principal productions are mud, dust and factory girls. The city proper, at least that part that I saw, consisted of a long, narrow entry, up one flight of stairs, adorned overhead with a frescoing of gas meters, and carpeted with worn out tobacco quids, and furnished with one chair, two settees, and as many huge, square packing cases, marked "Q. M. D." Scattered around this palatial entrance-hall were some forty or fifty conscripts, looking very much as if they expected to be exempted by reason of old age, before the young man with a ferocious moustache should notify them of their turn. Most of them, however, were doomed to disappointment, for while they counted the hours of delay, the door would suddenly open, and the tall young man would single out a man and march him through the open doorway, to be seen no more.

By-and-by—that is, after several hours waiting—my turn came.

"John Smith!" shouted the door-keeper.

"That's me," says I, and with a cheer from the crowd, I entered a large square room where two persons sat writing at a table, and a third, evidently the surgeon, was examining a man in the last stages of nudity.

One of the writers at the table, a young man with curly hair and blue eyes, nodded to me, and dipping his pen in the ink, commenced—

"John Smith, what's your name?"

"John Smith," says I.

"Where were you born?"

"Podunk, Maine."

"What did your great-grand-mother die of?"

"Darned if I know," says I.

"Call it hapentap," says he; "and your grand-father too?"

"I don't care what you call it," says I, for I was a little riled by his nonsensical questions.

"Did you ever have boils?" says he.

"Not a boil."

"Or fits?"

"Nary fit."

"Or delerium tremens?"

"No sir-ee!"

"Or rickets?"

"I'll ricket you," says I, for I thought he meant something else.

"Did you ever have the measles?" says he.

Here I took off my coat.

"Or the itch?"

"Yes sir, I—that ere fist (and I shoved a very large brown one within three inches of his nose) has been itching, for the last ten minutes, to knock your pesky head off, you little, mean, low-lived, contemptible whelp, you."

"My dear sir," said the mild-spoken gentlemanly surgeon, laying his hand on my arm; "calm yourself, I pray. Don't let your angry passions rise, but take off your clothes, so I can see what you are made of."

So I suppressed my anger, and withdrawing to a corner, I hung my clothes up on the floor, and presented myself for examination, clad only with the covering nature had given me, except about a square inch of court-plaster on my right shin, where I had fallen over a chair, the night before, feeling for a match.

"Young man," said the surgeon, looking me straight in the eye, "you have got the myopia."

"Yes, sir," said I, "and a good one, too—a little Bininger, with a drop of Stoughton, makes an excellent eye-opener, of a morning."

"And there seems to be an amaurotic tendency of the right eye, accompanied with opthalmia."

"Show!" says I.

"And that white spot in the left eye betokens a cataract."

"I guess you mean in the ear," says I, "cause I went in swimming this morning, and got an all-fired big bubble in my left ear," and here I jumped up and down two or three times on my left foot, but to no purpose. As soon as I stopped he mounted a chair and commenced feeling the top of my head.

"Was your family ever troubled with epilepsy?" says he.

"Only the two boys," says I; "when they catch them, my wife always goes at them with a fine tooth comb, the first thing."

Jumping off the chair he hit me a lick in the ribs that nearly knocked me over, and before I had time to remonstrate, his arms were round my neck and his head pressed against my bosom the same way that Sophia Ann does, when she wants me to buy her some new bonnets and things.

"Just what I thought," says he; "tuberculosis and hemoptysis, combined with a defect in the scapular membrane and incipient phthysis!"

"Heavens!" says I, "what's that?"

"And cardiac disease."

"No?" said I.

"And Pendardites!"

"Thunder!" said I.

"Stop talking! Now count after me—one!"

"One!" said I, dead with fright.

"Asthma! Two."

"Two," I yelled.

"Exotis of the right febular! Three."

"Three!" I gasped.

"Coxalgia! Four."

"Murder!" said I. "Four."

"Confirmed duodenum of the right ventricle! Five."

"Oh! doctor, ain't you most through? I feel faint!"

"Through? No! Not half through. Why, my friend, Pandora's box was nothing to your chest. You have sphynixiana, and gloriosis, and conchoilogia, and persiflage, and—"

Here my knees trembled so I leaned against the table for support.

"And permanent luxation of the anterior lobe of the right phalanx."

My only answer was a deprecatory gesture.

"And scrofulous diathesis and omnipodites."

I sank to the floor in utter despair.

"Elutriation!" he yelled, for he saw I was going fast—"and maxillarium and—"

From *Portrait Monthly of the New York Illustrated News*, Vol. 1, No. 5, November, 1863, p. 71, cols. 2-3.

From The Copperhead Catechism: For the Instruction of Such Politicians As Are of Tender Years, by Montgomery Wilson.

What is the chief aim of a Copperhead in this life?

The chief aim of a Copperhead is to abuse the President, vilify the Administration, and glorify himself before the people.

153

What is the purpose he will serve thereby?

He will thereby give assistance to his "friends" in the fulfillment of their desires.

To what end will such assistance lead?

To the uprooting of Abolitionism, the annihilation of Republicanism, the establishment of Copperheadism, the perpetration of a Peace, and the general display of Universal Submission.

How will abuse of the President and vilification of the administration lead thereto?

By making Foreign Nations believe that the North is distracted by dissection, while the South is pursuing its career in unison.

How does a Copperhead accomplish this?

By the blatancy of his utterances which he causes to be heard over every other sound, as the tones of a brazen trumpet are over those of a silver lute.

Wherein does a Copperhead glorify himself before the people?

By the assumption of an ardent devotion to the Goddess of Liberty, and by the liberal display of the language of departed statesmen.

My dear boy, what are the articles of thy belief?

I believe in One Country, One Constitution, One Destiny;

And in George B. McClellan, formerly General-in-Chief of the Armies of the United States; Who was born of respectable parents; Suffered under Edwin M. Stanton; Was refused reinforcements, and descended into the swamps of the Chickahominy; He was driven therefrom by fire and by sword, and upon the seventh day of battle ascended Malvern Hill, from whence he withdrew to Harrison's Landing, where he rested many days; He returned to the Potomac, fought the battle of Antietam, and was then removed from his high command, and entered into Oblivion; From this he shall one day arise and be elevated to the Presidential chair, there to dispense his favors unto all who follow.

Who is Captain Semmes?

A noted sea-dog whose barque we are unable to see, but whose bite we are too often able to feel.

Who is James Buchanan?

An "Old Public Functionary," who, before his sands of political life ran out, placed his country in a pickle, and was afterwards sent up Salt River by the people.

Who is Governor Seymour?

A "friend" who promised to test the legality of the Conscription, but was "brought up" by the Habeas Corpus.

Who is Vallandigham?

A politician who overstepped the mark and found himself beyond the border.

What is Fort LaFayette?

A round residence for those who do not act on the square.

On what ground does Fernando the Gothamite claim the right to be your leader?

Because "solitary and alone" he put the *bawl* of Peace in motion.

What is a Copperhead's peace?

A scarecrow in the plumage of a dove.

What is the banner of peace?

The flag of many stripes and but few stars.

VII
Valentines

In the war-torn United States of the eighteen-sixties, St. Valentine's Day was still celebrated by lovers North and South through the centuries-old custom of exchanging love messages.

This custom is believed to have originated with the pagan festival of the Lupercalia which took place on February 14 and 15 in ancient Rome, commemorating the rural god Faunus and the goddess Juno Regina. As part of this celebration the young people drew names from a bowl or urn to determine who would be their beloved for the coming year. The couples thus paired off had to exchange gifts and promise to remain true to each other until the next Lupercalia.

With the advent of Christianity, many such early Roman and Greek festivals were turned into Christian feasts, and it is quite likely that the pagan Lupercalia became the Christian St. Valentine's Day honoring the memory of the martyred priest Valentinus, or Valentine.

In 270 A.D., the Emperor Claudius II, who was constantly waging war, issued an edict prohibiting new marriages to be entered into by the young people. It was his theory that married men would not be eager to fight. Valentine, the Roman Catholic priest, on the other hand, believed that the mating of young people should be blessed by marriage, and despite the emperor's edict, continued to marry those who came to him. When Claudius learned of the priest's disobedience he ordered him to be imprisoned and, later, beheaded, supposedly on February 14.

155

A popular pertinent legend associated with this patron saint of lovers is that while he was awaiting execution, he befriended the jailor's blind daughter and restored her sight just before his death. It is said that he wrote the girl a farewell note and signed it "From your Valentine," an expression since used on greeting cards by millions of lovers.

St. Valentine's Day became very popular in England, where the first love messages are believed to date back to the days of Chaucer, and the custom of drawing names or valentines, as they were later called, from an urn, persisted until the time of the famous diarist Samuel Pepys. All such early valentines, both abroad and in America, were handmade, and eighteenth century lovers who found poetry writing a difficult task welcomed a handbook published in 1797 entitled *The Young Man's Valentine Writer*.

England produced the first commercial valentines, but in the 1840's the vogue spread to the United States, where Esther A. Howland, of Worcester, Massachusetts, inspired by a valentine sent to her stationer father, became this country's first valentine publisher. Others followed her and before long American printers had developed a flourishing trade in this field. Over three million valentines were sold in 1847, with sentimental ones outvaluing the comics. Sales for 1857 amounted to a quarter of a million dollars. By 1858 there were five important producers of valentines, two in New York and three in New England, with salesmen traveling through the West and South.

The sale of valentines did not diminish during the Civil War; if anything it increased for neither the attack on Fort Donelson, nor the siege of Vicksburg, nor the command slogan from the *New York Tribune* to go "On to Richmond" could make the young people of the sixties forget to send a valentine to their beloved on February 14. Many publishers of valentines directed their advertisements to the attention of the soldiers. The American Valentine Company offered "Soldier valentine packets, Army valentine packets, New Military comic valentines, Torch of love packets," etc. The fancy, fussy, and expensive multiple-layer valentine, so typical of the ornate and overdone decoration of the Victorian era, made its appearance in the 1860's with gilt trimmings, little mirrors, silver lace, inserts of chiffon and satin-finish paper. There was an abundance of penny valentines, too, replete with patriotic catch phrases of the day.

While a great many Civil War love messages were sentimental, a greater proportion, like the cartoons of the period, were concerned with leading issues and events. Lovemaking took on a social significance in topical comic valentines. These were often so caustic, highly critical, and uncomplimentary to the recipient that they remained unsigned.

"Who will my true love be?" is the age-old question asked on lovers' day. After reading some of the comic valentines, the appropriate reply would seem to be "No one. No one." But perhaps if there had been no love in the sender's heart there would have been no bitterness either.

Be My Valentine.

. . . Cupid in Blue and Gray shot a few poisonous darts at nineteenth century lovers. . . .

There were endless caricatures of men on the political and military scene . . . the flamboy-ant officer . . . the cowardly soldier and officer . . . the abolitionist . . . the secessionist . . . and war profiteers.

Ah! what is the matter, my trooper so gay,
    While to this young lass you are kneeling?
Your head, it is soft—as for heart you have none.
    Your butt alone seems to have feeling.

Swaggering like some great high-grandee,
How d'ye do, my Soldier Dandy;
The girls, you think, no doubt get sweet
On you as you strut through the street.
But they're more apt to think you scamp,
When you're found roaming from your camp

513

Unlike the cartoons of the day, political valentines were rather simple and unclut-
tered. They contained no balloons, in which the printing is often difficult to de-
cipher, and rarely featured more than two figures in a picture. In four lines of
verse or more, the sarcastic point of criticism was directed at the victim's heart
with the accuracy of cupid's arrow.

THE CAPTAIN.

When duty calls, I hope you'll be
Not hid behind some friendly tree
But leading on the gallant line
To win the fight and a Valentine.

159

THE COLONEL.

When perched on your charger on dress parade
   You looked as brave soldier as ever was made
If you look but as brave when the bullets fly
   Your Country will love you and so will I.

A. Wrigley, Publisher, 27 Chatham Street N. Y.

TO A ZOUAVE.

Zu-Zu, you made a splendid run,
From Bull-Run fight, to Washington;
Your time was good and can't be bea
By Bully Runners e'er so fleet;
Your frats of logs, such wonders raised,
That every one has stood amazed ;
So coward Kbcreant, Renegade,
Your Valentine I'll not be made.

The regiment of Zouaves had been recruited by Elmer Elsworth from the volunteer fire departments of New York City. Heavy-shouldered, hard-faced and spoiling for a fight, the Zouaves were dressed in gray, scarlet and blue Zouave uniforms and carried rifles and huge bowie knives. Looked upon by Washingtonians as a gang of roughnecks, they were spoiling for battle, convinced that they could wipe out the Rebels in short order. The First Battle of Bull Run proved otherwise and sadly demonstrated that it required more than bravado to win a battle. After the retreat to Washington, only a "gaudy handful" of Fire Zouaves had managed to survive the first great battle of the war.

A REBEL.

To trample on "our dear Old Flag",
   You rashly did attempt;
The Valentine most met for you,
   Is a *Neck-tie made of Hemp.*

162

A REGULAR.

My love is a regular man—
A man with a regular way;
He means to regulate me—if he can,
When he gets his regular pay.
But I'll be no regular's wife,
No! no! not for all creation;
For who could enjoy married life,
When bound to a mere regulation.

163

SOLDIER.

You are a gallant soldier,
    With a splendid figure for parade ;
The country is safe in your keeping,
    So long as you fight in the shade.
I fancy myself *your* beloved !
    Would'nt you have a jolly good time ?
I'd make you stand guard over a cradle,
    And do double duty to Valentine

N. Y. Union Valentine Co., No. 134 William St., N. Y.

COPPERHEAD.

Of all things whom honorable men despise,
  The meanest is the copperhead and traitor,
Whose presence is a libel on our liberties,
  And his thoughts a libel on his Creator.
Anathema Marantha ! Let him be accursed :
  Let him drink of the poison he distils :
Let him be marked of enemies the worst,
  That has brought on the Republic all its ills.
The woman would be branded with ever living shame,
Who, for a Valentine, breathed a copperhead's name.

N. Y. Union Valentine Co., No. 134 William St., N. Y.

A Candidate for Military Promotion.

I was tired of the ranks, and promoted I'd be,
I tho't the shoulder straps would look finely on me,
But when I applied, it was only to find,
The promotion before just hurt me behind.

On to Richmond.

"*On to Richmond!*" now's the call :
  Rally, rally, great and small :
  Oh ! by goily, how they'll scoot,
  When they see you, *raw recruit*.

At almost the very outset of the war, the masthead of Horace Greeley's Tribune
bore the slogan "On To Richmond." Greeley's goal was not achieved until 1865.
The sender of this valentine sarcastically implies that the Southerners will hardly
be likely to retreat before this raw recruit.

Ha, ha ! don't you think you're brave ?
No officer e're looked *bolder*,
But, all who march with you,
Think the asses head should be upon your shoulder.

Home Guard.

You enlist! not to fight at your *dear* country's call.
You keep from the field where the brave fight & fall ;
A *sneak* and a *coward*, and no force or persuasion,
Could make you leave home, but the fact of *invasion*.

TO A DRAGOON.

"Bring forth the steed! the steed was brought,"
And on his back to mount you thought;
But don't you think for a Dragoon,
That you commenced almost too soon?
Before you bade the ground good bye,
Why did you not a hobby try?

A Reconnoiterer.

You were sent as a scout to try to discover,
If the enemy's troops were crossing the river,
But your eyes are engaged with the girl on the fence,
While the dog does the duty of *reckon-ı-scents*.

Abolition Philanthropist.

O, massa Abolitionist! you're mighty fond of jokes,
And play em on de *darkey* as well as on white folks;
But all your mighty promises dey neber come to pass,
And every time we take your chair de burs stick in
our——trouserloons.

In every army, great and small,
   There is a set of patent *blowers*,
Who of the work make out to shirk all,
   And of their valiant deeds are *crowers*.
But let a battle once commence,
   Away they travel for some tree or fence ;
You find their brains too soon are addled,
   And you've but to see that they've *skedaddled*.

QUARTERMASTER.

You fat old cuss, give us our grub,
You have our cash to feed us,
You're paid to keep us in good trim,
And not to *sponge* and *bleed* us.

The officer who paid for his commission

Charge boys, charge, while I stand behind a tree ;
The fighting is for you, and it's left for me to see.
I suppose you will ask me how I got my position,
I hauled out my money and paid for my commission.

The Secessionist.

You are the man who chuckles when the news
    Comes o'er the wires, and tells of sad disaster :
Pirates on sea succeeding—burning ships and crews,
    Rebels on land marauding, thicker, aye, and faster,
You are the two-faced villain, though not very bold,
Who would barter your country for might or for gold.

War profiteers did a thriving business during the four bloody years of war. From the very outset, when word had come from Baltimore of the attack on the Sixth Massachusetts Regiment, and it appeared that Washington was in danger, there was a short-lived fear of famine. Speculating grocers quickly raised the price of flour from seven and one-half dollars to twelve and fifteen dollars a barrel. In late 1861, Stanton cleared the swindling contractors from the War Department and new uniforms for the soldiers were made of wool instead of shoddy. But the grafters always found a way back. The frauds and thievery in the Commissary Department persisted. Salt pork floating in fat was served to the sick in the hospitals until Annie Wittemyer of Iowa introduced her special diet for the sick in 1863. During the siege of Vicksburg, when cars and transports did get through to the men at Young's Point, they were usually so crowded and filthy and the starved animals in such an unhealthy condition that many of the regiments chose salt rations of the army in preference to unsanitary fresh meat. Tainted meat found its way to every battlefront to the advantage of some ruthless profiteer.

SHODDY.

You can't see it?   No wonder you can't,
   With a fifty dollar green back in your eye;
The soldier may starve—the sailor may want,
   What cares Shoddy if even they die?
He's a curse to his kind—his country's worst bane,
   Deserving the noose on the hangman's line;
But, alas, *you* don't get it, and to publish *your* shame,
   Is left alone for this poor Valentine.

N. Y. Union Valentine Co., No. 134 William St., N. Y.

TO THE SURGEON.

Ho! ho! old saw bones, here you come,
Yes, when the rebels whack us.
You are always ready with your traps,
To mangle, saw, and hack us.

At the outset of the war there was an acute shortage of surgeons. Many were young, unskilled, and only partially trained. Some had no preparation other than a quick course in military surgery. Others relied on pamphlets which were hastily prepared to act as a guide. There were strict rules concerning amputations, for example, which this valentine refers to. "Amputate with as little delay as possible," advised one handbook on surgery.

Bibliography

Abernethy, Thomas Perkins. *The Burr Conspiracy.* New York, 1954.

Adams, Ephraim Douglass. *Great Britain and the American Civil War.* New York, 1925.

Adams, Francis Colburn. *Siege of Washington, D.C.: Written Expressly for Little People.* New York, 1867.

Adams, James Truslow. *America's Tragedy.* New York and London, 1934.

Alcott, Louisa May. *Hospital Sketches.* Boston, 1863.

American Rebellion—Report of the Speeches of the Rev. Henry Ward Beecher Delivered at Public Meetings. Manchester, 1864.

"Anecdotes of General Garfield," *Portrait Monthly of the New York Illustrated News,* I (January, 1864),103.

"Anecdotes of General Grant," *Portrait Monthly of The New York Illustrated News,* I (December, 1863), 86.

Battles and Leaders of the Civil War. 4 vols. New York, 1956.

Becker, Stephen D. *Comic Art in America.* New York, 1959.

Beiger, Joseph, and Beiger, Dorothy (eds.). *Diary of America.* New York, 1957.

Bill, Alfred Hoyt. *The Beleaguered City, Richmond 1861-65.* New York, 1946.

Blada, V. (pseud.). *Confederate War Etchings. (1862-1863).* London, 1863.   "Sketches from the Civil War in North America, 1861, '62, '63," *Magazine of History,* Extra No. 60, 1917, 222-242.

Blair, Walter, *Native American Humor (1800-1900)*. New York and Chicago, 1937.

Boykin, Edward C. *Ghost Ship of the Confederacy*. New York, 1957.

Bremmer, Ellen. "Orpheus C. Kerr," *Civil War History*, II (September, 1956), 121-129.

Brock, Miss Sally A. (pseud. Virginia Madison) ed. *The Southern Amaranth*. New York, 1869. Poem, "Cutting off the Buttons," p. 401.

Brooks, Noah. *Washington in Lincoln's Time*. New York, 1895.

Browne, Charles Farrar. *Artemus Ward, His Book*. New York, 1864.

Bruere, Martha Bensley, and Beard, Mary Ritter. *Laughing Their Way—Women's Humor in America*. New York, 1934.

Burr, Frank A., and Hinton, Richard J. *"Little Phil" and His Troopers*: *The Life of General Philip Sheridan*. Providence, 1888.

Burton, Margaret Davis. *The Woman Who Battled for the Boys in Blue: Mother Bickerdyke*. San Francisco, 1886.

Carpenter, F. B. *Six Months in the White House*. New York, 1867.

Carpenter, George M. *History of the Eighth Regiment Vermont Volunteers*. Boston, 1886.

Catton, Bruce. *This Hallowed Ground*. Garden City, N.Y., 1951.   . *Glory Road*. Garden City, N.Y., 1952.   *A Stillness at Appomattox*. Garden City, N.Y., 1956.

Chamberlain, James D. (ed.). *The Romance of Greeting Cards*. London, 1956.

Chase, Julia. *Mary A. Bickerdyke, "Mother."* Lawrence, Kans., 1896.

Chestnut, Mary Boykin. *A Diary from Dixie*. New York, 1905.

Christie, Anne M. "Bill Arp," *Civil War History*, II (September, 1956), 103-119.

Confederate Scrap-Book. Richmond, 1893.

Corley, Florence Fleming. *Confederate City, Augusta, Georgia, 1860-65*. Columbia, S.C., 1960.

"Copperheads," *Magazine of History*, Extra No. 58, 1917, 83-117.

Curtis, Orson B.A.M. *History of the Twenty-Fourth Michigan of the Iron Brigade*. Detroit, 1891.

Dannett, Sylvia G. L. *Noble Women of the North*. New York, 1959.

Davis, Burke. *Our Incredible Civil War*. New York, 1960.

DeLeon, T. C. *Belles, Beaux and Brains of the 60's*. New York, 1909.

Diary of Gideon Welles. Boston and New York, 1909.

Dodge, T. A. *A Bird's-Eye View of Our Civil War*. Boston and New York, 1883.

Drepperd, Carl W. *Early American Prints*. New York and London, 1930.

Dryden, Charles. *War in the Midst of America From A Near Point of View*. London, 1864.

Elliott, Charles Winslow. *Winfield Scott, the Soldier and the Man*. New York, 1937.

Emerson, Marion W. "Hearts and Darts," *Avocations*, I (February, 1938), 414-418.

"An Examination of Military Position," *Portrait Monthly of the New York Illustrated News,* I (April, 1864), 155.

Frank Leslie's Illustrated Newspaper, 1861-1865.

Fiske, John. *The Mississippi Valley in the Civil War.* Boston and New York, 1900.

Glyndon, Howard (pseud.). *Idyls of Battle.* New York, 1865.

Gordon, Armistead C. *Memories and Memorials of William Gordon McCabe.* Richmond, 1925.

Gray, Wood. *The Hidden Civil War; The Story of the Copperheads.* New York, 1942.

Halpine, Charles Graham. *The Life and Adventures, Songs, Services and Speeches of Private Miles O'Reilly (Forty-Seventh Regiment, New York Volunteers).* New York, 1864.

Harper's New Monthly Magazine, (December, 1865).

Harper's Pictorial History of the Great Rebellion New York, 1866.

Harper's Weekly, 1861-1865.

Hassler, Warren W. *General George B. McClellan: Shield of the Union.* Baton Rouge, 1957.

Hereford, Elizabeth J. *Rebel Rhymes and Other Poems.* New York, 1898.

Hills, Alfred C. Macpherson, *The Great Confederate Philosopher and Southern Blower.* New York, 1864.

Hinman, Wilbur F. *Corporal Si Klegg and His "Pard."* Cleveland, 1887.

Hodgson, Mrs. Willowghby. "Valentines," *Antiques,* XVII (February, 1930), 145-149.

Holzman, Robert S. *Stormy Ben Butler.* New York, 1954.

Horn, Stanley F. *The Army of Tennessee.* Indianapolis and New York. 1941.

"How I Passed the Doctor, An Incident During the Draft," *Portrait Monthly of The New York Illustrated News,* I (November, 1863), 71.

Howe, Julia Ward. *Reminiscences—1819-1899.* Boston and New York, 1899.

Hubbell, Jay Broadus. *The South in American Literature 1607-1900.* Durham, 1954.

Hutchinson, Ruth, .and Adams, Ruth. *Every Day's a Holiday.* New York, 1951.

Jordan, Donaldson, and Pratt, Edwin J. *Europe and the American Civil War.* Boston and New York. 1931.

Kelsey, D. M. *Deeds of Daring by Both Blue and Gray.* Philadelphia, St. Louis, and San Francisco, 1884.

Kirkland, Edward C. *The Peacemakers of 1864.* New York, 1927.

Kirkland, Frazar (pseud.). *The Book of Anecdotes of the War of the Rebellion.* 2 vols. Hartford, 1866.

Kouwenenhoven, John A. *The Columbia Historical Portrait of New York.* New York, 1953.

Lee, Ruth Webb. *A History of Valentines.* New York and London, 1952.

Leech, Margaret. *Reveille in Washington, 1860-1865.* New York, 1941.

Leland, C. G., and Leland, H. P. *Ye Book of Copperheads*. Philadelphia, 1863.

Letters of Major Jack Downing (pseud.) of the Downingville Militia. New York, 1864.

Lewisohn, Ludwig. *Expression in America*. New York, 1932.

Life in the South from the Commencement of the War by a Blockaded British Subject from the Spring of 1860 to August 1862. London, 1863.

L'Illustration, 1860-1865.

Livermore, Mary. *My Story of the War*. Hartford, 1890.   *The Story of My Life*. Hartford, 1897.

Lucid, Robert F. "Anecdotes and Recollections," *Civil War History*, II (September, 1956), 29-48.

Lyman, Susan E. "Nineteenth Century Valentines," *Museum of the City of New York Bulletin*, I (February, 1938), 30-31.

McDonald, Cornelia. *A Diary with Reminiscences of the War and Refugee Life in the Shenandoah Valley 1860-1865*. Nashville, 1935.

Magill, Mary Tucker. *Women, or Chronicles of the Late War*. Baltimore, 1871.

Major Jack Downing. Northern Humor. London, 1867.

Martineau, Harriet. *Society in America*. New York, 1837.

Mason, Emily V. *The Southern Poems of the War: War Songs and Poems of the Southern Confederacy*. Baltimore, 1867.

Mason, Virginia. *The Public Life and Private Correspondence of James M. Mason*. Roanoke, Va., 1903.

Matthews, Albert. "Origin of Butternut and Copperhead." (Publications of the Colonial Society of Massachusetts, Vol. XX, pp. 205-237.) Boston, 1920.

Matthews, Mitford M. (ed.). *A Dictionary of Americanisms*. Chicago, 1951.

Mears, C. G. Alton. "Will You Be Mine, Oh Valentine!" *Hobbies*, XXXI (No. 7), 27-30.

Miers, Earl Schenck. *The Great Rebellion: The Emergence of the American Conscience*. Cleveland, 1958.

Miller, Francis Trevelyan (ed.). *Photographic History of the Civil War*. New York, 1911.

Monaghan, James. *Civil War on the Western Border 1854-1865*. Boston, 1955.

Moore, Frank. *Women of the War—Their Heroism and Self-Sacrifice*. Hartford, 1866.
    . *The Civil War in Song and Story: 1860-1865*. New York, 1889.
    . (ed.). *The Rebellion Record*. New York, 1864.

Murrell, William. *A History of American Graphic Humor*. 2 vols. New York, 1938.

Nardin, James T. "The War in *Vanity Fair*," *Civil War History*, II (September, 1956), 67-85.

Nasby, Petroleum (pseud.). *The Nasby Papers*. Indianapolis, 1864.

Nevins, Allan. *The War for the Union*. New York, 1959.

Newell, Robert Henry. *The Orpheus C. Kerr Papers*. New York, 1862, 1865.

Nichols, Roy G. *The Stakes of Power 1845-1877*. New York, 1961.

"A Nosegay of Valentines," *American Heritage*, VI (February, 1955), 62-65.

Parton, James. *Caricature and Other Comic Art in All Times and in Many Lands*. New York, 1877.

Patrick, Robert W. *Knapsack and Rifle; Or, Life in the Grand Army*. Boston, 1887.

Phisterer, Frederick. *New York in the War of the War of the Rebellion 1861 to 1865*. Albany, 1912.

The Phunny Phellow, 1862, 1863.

Pollard, Edward. *The Lost Cause*. New York, 1866.

Pollard, Edward A. *A Southern History of the War; The Last Year of the War*. New York, 1866.

Pollard, Julia Cuthbert. *Richmond's Story*. Richmond, 1954.

Poore, Ben. *Perley's Reminiscences or Sixty Years in the National Metropolis*. Philadelphia, 1886.

Porter, Admiral David Dixon. *Incidents and Anecdotes of the Civil War*. New York, 1886.

Pratt, Fletcher. *Ordeal by Fire: An Informal History of the Civil War*. New York, 1935.

"The President (Lincoln) on Kissing," *Portrait Monthly of The New York Illustrated News*, I (April, 1864), 155.

Punch, or *The London Charivari*, 1860-1865.

Quinn, Arthur Hobson (ed.). *The Literature of the American People: An Historical and Critical Survey*. New York, 1951.

Reed, Charles W. *Hardtack and Coffee*. Boston, 1887.

Reed, John Q. "Artemus Ward," *Civil War History*, II (September, 1956), 87-101.

Rourke, Constance. *American Humor*. New York, 1931.

Russell, Sir William Howard. *My Diary North and South*. New York, 1954.

Sasscier, Agnes L. "Valentines. First Aid to the Lovelorn," *American Collector*, VIII (February, 1939), 10-11.

. "Sentiments of the Valentine," *Hobbies*, LXII (February, 1958), 28-29, 60.

. "St. Valentine, King of Hearts," *Hobbies*, LXIII (February, 1959), 58-59, 64, 67.

Seitz, Don C. *Artemus Ward (Charles Farrar Browne): A Biography and a Bibliography*. New York and London, 1919.

Sheridan, Philip M. *Personal Memo*. New York, 1888.

Smith, Charles Henry. *Bill Arp's Peace Papers*. New York, 1873.

"The Soldier and the Lady," *Portrait Monthly of The New York Illustrated News*, I (January, 1864), 110.

Southern Confederate Medical Journal, XXIII (October, 1830).

Southern Punch, 1860-1865.

Stern, Philip Van Doren. *They Were There.* New York, 1959.

Stine, J. H. *History of the Army of the Potomac.* Philadelphia, 1892.

Taylor, Mary. *Unpublished Diary of Mary Taylor.* Handley Library, Winchester, Virginia.

Trefousse, Hans L. *Ben Butler; The South Called Him Beast!* New York, 1957.

Trent, William Peterfield, *et al* (eds.). *The Cambridge History of American Literature.* 3 vols. New York, 1891.

Vanity Fair, 1859-1863.

Vandiver, Frank. *Mighty Stonewall.* New York, 1957.

Victor, Orville J. *The History, Civil, Political and Military, of the Southern Rebellion.* New York, 1863.

The War of the Rebellion: *A Compilation of the Official Records of the Union and Confederate Armies.* Washington, 1880.

"Washington in 1861," *Magazine of American History,"* XII (July, 1884).

"Washington on the Eve of the War," *Century Magazine,* XXVI (July, 1883).

Wecter, Dixon. *The Saga of American Society*: *A Record of Social Aspiration, 1607-1937.* New York, 1937.

Weil, Elma Allee, and Knittle, Rhea Mansfield. "The Vagaries of the Valentine," *The Antiquarian,* VIII (February, 1927), 30-34.

Weiss, Harry B. "A Brief History of American Jest Books," *Bulletin of the New York Public Library,* XLVII (April, 1943), 273-289.

. "English and American Valentine Writers," *Ibid.,* XLIII (February, 1939), 71-86.

. "Preliminary Checklist of Valentine Writers," *Ibid.,* pp. 77-86.

Weitenkamp, Frank. *A Century of Political Cartoons*: *Caricature in the United States from 1800 to 1900.* New York, 1944.

Whitman, Walt. *The Complete Poetry and Prose.* New York, 1948.

Williams, Thomas Harry. *Lincoln and His Generals.* New York, 1952.

Wilson, Montgomery. *The Copperhead Catechism.* New York, 1864.

Worthington, C. J. *The Woman in Battle.* Hartford, 1876.

Wright, William P. *War of 1861-1865.* Unpublished.

DATE DUE

GAYLORD			PRINTED IN U.S.A.